JAMBO, KILIMANJARO!

A Mid-Life
African Adventure

Marilyn Kay Wilson Weaver

Jambo, Kilimanjaro! A Mid-Life African Adventure

Scripture taken from the HOLY BIBLE, NEW INTERNATIONAL VERSION. Copyright © 1973, 1978, 1984 International Bible Society. Used by permission of Zondervan Bible Publishers. (NIV)

Scripture taken from the New King James Version. Copyright © 1982 by Thomas Nelson, Inc. Used by permission. All rights reserved. (NKJV)

Unless otherwise noted, Scripture quotations are from the King James Version. (KJV)

Endorsements for *Jambo*, Kilimanjaro!

We have known Marilyn and her husband, Terry Weaver, more than ten years. I and my wife have worked closely with them for more than five years. Marilyn has worked diligently in training women in Tanzania to realize their position in Christ. Many of them have grown up spiritually and are serving the body of Christ as pastors, teachers, evangelists and other church leadership positions. Training of pastors at Kilimanjaro Christian College has brought tremendous change in their marriages and families and reflected in many Christian homes. **Lazaro and Eli Kiriama—Principal and Dean of Kilimanjaro Christian College, Moshi, Tanzania**

Marilyn Weaver has painted wonderful word pictures of the challenges, the spontaneity, the beauty, the tragedies, the humor and the power of God all present in East Africa. Stories told with a warm sense of humor, illustrates to readers how wonderfully God can use those who are simply willing to say "yes," and go for Him. "It's not by might, not by power, but by His Spirit" is a truth that is told page after page of this book. Entertaining, informative, and challenging are words that I would use to describe this book. I recommend it. **Tom Brazell—Director of International Ministries, Elim Fellowship, Lima, NY**

I hope and trust that many, both young and old, will read and enjoy this thrilling and exhilarating story. You will feel like you are on an African adventure with them! You will be greatly encouraged and challenged. This true story is made more real to me, having been with Terry and Marilyn in Tanzania twice and observed and experienced their love for the people, their battle with both spiritual and cultural darkness and personal hardship and challenge. The Lord gave them wisdom, perseverance, and ultimate victory with abundant eternal fruit. The Weavers are truly unsung heroes who have poured out their lives for the people of Tanzania. They are people of integrity, vision, and a spiritual father and mother to many. May God continue to use them to change lives; I know He has used them to change mine. **Andy Zack— Executive Associate Pastor, Love Joy Church, Lancaster, NY**

Table of Contents

Introduction

Even when I wasn't the least bit interested in the guidance of God; He was profoundly interested in directing my life. His plan began to unfold when I was a preschooler. Unfortunately, I let my personal desires get in the way of God's perfect plan. Having made a mess of my life, at thirty I made a decision for Christ. A great transition followed. By forty I had a massive encounter with the Holy Spirit, and by the time I was fifty, the ministry planted in my heart at around the age of five took root. *But may the God of all grace, who called us to His eternal glory by Christ Jesus, after you have suffered a while, perfect, establish, strengthen, and settle you.* (1 Peter 5:10)

God is faithful; He never gave up on me or His plan for me. Continually He intervened at decisive moments. In college during the first semester, when I was free from the restraints of parents, mercifully, I met my future husband, Terry. He, too, was far from the Lord but with a call of God on his life. *For the LORD Almighty has purposed, and who can thwart him?* (Isa. 14:27 NIV) When finally at thirty we surrendered to God's call, the Holy Spirit graciously began the process of restoring our souls and changing our rebellious, selfish attitudes. *The LORD will perfect that which concerns me; Your mercy, O LORD, endures forever.* (Psalm 138:8NKJV) He then engineered the next twenty years in preparation for His highest purpose for us! After suffering years of depression, I was miraculously set free to proclaim His praises. His faithful intervention was transforming my life, renewing my mind and giving birth to my God-ordained purpose. ⚜

Jambo, Kilimanjaro! is the thrilling firsthand account of Father God's faithfulness in guiding and directing our lives during a decade of living in East Africa. Continually we witnessed the Lord's faithful intervention to provide us with ways of escape in the midst of horrific trials—whether under siege in a village or reaching hostile tribes. As we persisted in prayer, God was faithful to perform His Word and miraculous things happened. Faithfully the Lord dissolved religious traditions and transformed hearts to prepare the way for the founding of a Women's Bible College. Inspired by God's grace in our own lives, we went to Tanzania believing "God is Who He says He is and does what He says He will do!" And we were willing to tell the world about our faithful God!

Dedication

First and foremost to Jesus, who never gave up on me.

Secondly with a grateful heart, *Jambo, Kilimanjoro* is dedicated to all who prayed and gave to make it all possible.

To our children who sacrificed so we could go. With love to Eric and Elizabeth and Brian and Janine, and especially to our beloved grandchildren: Abigail Marianne, Olivia Grace, Nathaniel Joshua, and any others to come—this is the history of your grandparents, *Babu* and *Bibi Weaver.*

With special thanks to Terry, my wonderful husband, and Bonnie Kyle, a devoted new friend, both, who read and reread the manuscript, for their anointed advice and patience with me.

Prologue

During Vacation Bible School one summer, a seed for missions was dropped into my young heart. Around the table we preschoolers gathered, eyes wide open, gawking at the pictures of some dark skinned people—Ethiopians. They were so beautiful; I had never seen people of color. Smiling white teeth shined on their black faces. The women wore huge, baggy white dresses lovingly made by a culture who must have envisioned a people group with some meat on them. Our charge—roll bandages for them. Eagerly our chubby young fingers did our part. It was the beginning of a call to Africa. That was the summer I decided I would be a missionary; that was the year I fell in love with Jesus. I was so committed to my missionary vision that by the time I was in seventh grade, it was listed on my permanent record in the Bethel Park Public School that I, Marilyn Kay Wilson, would be a missionary teacher.

Then life happened. The destructive pubescent years turned my thinking upside down; my goals changed. The good news is that early in my collegiate experience I met my husband, Terry. Although we were far from God, we had embraced our parents' principles and married during the summer following our sophomore year. In the fall of 1966, drugs hit the college big time. Being married, we were independent of the crashing campus life. God's unseen hand was protecting us, even though spiritually we were becoming more and more distant from Him. To Terry, scientific knowledge and religion seemed incompatible. We were on track with our careers: I was teaching school and he was a grad student in microbiology at

3

A Ohio State. It was our plan our way. When the draft notice for Vietnam came, terror struck our hearts! Surely Christian parents and grandparents were praying for us; we spent the next twenty months on US soil. A

A God's hand guided our lives when we knew Him not. The Army interruption opened the way for the GI Bill to finance a PhD in microbiology. Decades later, that knowledge would be the key to opening the hearts of the unreached Barbaiq tribe south of the Serengeti Plains. One day while Terry was in the region holding a livestock clinic, God got the herdsmen's attention. Meds could help all the animals but one, which had a lethal viral disease. When Terry laid hands on the cow, God miraculously healed it. Eagerly the Barbaiq then asked about a God who healed cows! *wow* – A

We returned to Columbus after Terry's Army stint, and our son, Eric Matthew, was born in 1971. A year and half later the three of us moved to Ithaca, New York, where Terry began his academic career as a Cornell University professor. Although the Lord was mercifully continuing to order our steps, we thought we had no need of Him as we were living large the American dream—a great job, our first house, and another baby boy, named Brian Wilson. Our independent hearts were deceived by Ivy League pride and academic success. By the time we were thirty, our godless lives had spiraled downward. Eric was four and a half and Brian was one. Bold commitment to those beautiful sons reversed our self-centered focus and strengthened our resolve to work things out. *Being confident of this very thing, that He who has begun a good work in you will complete it until the day of Jesus Christ.* (Phil. 1:6 NKJV) A A

4

We returned to the church where I had first met Jesus and where we had been married ten years earlier. One day during an intense marriage counseling session, Pastor Dennis leaned over his desk and said, "I sense the power of the Holy Spirit in our midst. Let's go to the altar to pray." As he prayed over me, in my brokenness I spoke these words from my heart, "Jesus, I've made a mess of my life. I give it to You. See what you can do with it." God's light overcame the darkness of those days as we both recommitted our lives to Christ and surrendered to make Him the Lord of our lives. We felt compelled by God to leave Ithaca. God says He will *...give them beauty for ashes, the oil of joy for mourning, the garment of praise for the spirit of heaviness; that they may be called trees of righteousness, the planting of the Lord, that He may be glorified.*(Isa. 61:3 NKJV) And indeed He did!

We moved our family to New Jersey. Terry became the head of a biochemical research group. I enrolled in Philadelphia College of the Bible to fulfill my desire to know the One whose hand was faithfully guiding our lives. While in New Jersey, we were introduced to the *Old Time Gospel Hour.* One Sunday night, while watching the program, Terry felt the call of God to go help the fledgling Christian college. Off to Lynchburg we went, and for seven years we were actively involved in the foundational years of what is today Liberty University. We thought our sole purpose was to help, but God was also orchestrating the circumstances to further our understanding and knowledge of Him. While there, God gave Terry this scripture: *For the vision is yet for an appointed time; but at the end it will speak, and it will not lie. Though it tarries, wait for it; because it will surely come. It will not tarry.* (Hab. 2:3 NKJV)

Wow.—

5

Our love for God and the desire to grow in His grace and knowledge was fulfilled as we studied under the anointed Bible teacher, Dr. Harold Willmington. Such godly men as Dr. Ron Hawkins and Dr. Elmer Towns further inspired me as I prepared for a master's degree in Christian counseling. All that those men sowed into us would one day be reproduced through us to thousands in East Africa. The unseen faithful God was continually on the move molding our lives. We eventually left Liberty and returned to the New York State University system, where Terry became the Dean of Agriculture and Allied Health at State University of New York (SUNY) at Alfred, NY. During that time I was back in God's school. After a powerful encounter with the Holy Spirit, I voraciously devoured every book I could on the gifts of the Spirit. I had met the Spirit of Christ in a new and awesome way and would *never* be the same. *and was - neither have I really -*

Two years later we settled in Fredonia, a small town in western New York that was home to Fredonia State University, where Terry held the position of chairman of biology. There we promised our sons we would not move again until they finished school, and we didn't. We had no idea what God's *vision* was for the future, but we were learning to experience His grace and faithfulness along the way. In every area of life, He was preparing us for His future work. Surely He had redeemed my mess and my soul! *

"For I know the plans I have for you," declares the LORD, "plans to prosper you and not to harm you, plans to give you hope and a future. Then you will call upon me and come and pray to me, and I will listen to you. You will seek me and find me when you seek

*me with all your heart. I will be found by you," declares the LORD,
"and will bring you back from captivity." (Jer. 29:11-14 NIV)*

There is no shame in waiting for the seed God deposits in your
spirit to germinate, blossom, and then bring forth fruit.
Looking back, I have been grateful for the years of waiting as
the unseen hand of God tilled the soil—plowing it under again
and again. The greater the wisdom, the fewer disastrous
mistakes; the more trials, the more perseverance—and I was
about to need plenty of both.

We Are Going Where?

We had just returned to our hotel room following Brian's graduation from Zion Bible Institute. As I closed my suitcase, I clearly heard the Holy Spirit speak to me and say *"This is the way your life is going to be."* I had no idea what it meant. Carefully, I tucked His words in my heart. The year was 1996; it was forty-five years after the original seed for missions had been deposited in my heart during Vacation Bible School. God was about to water that seed!

Back home from Zion, we packed Brian for his missions trip to Slovakia. Eric was occupied at Syracuse with his graduate studies and Terry's semester was finished at Fredonia. Even though it was May, ice floes could still be seen floating on Lake Erie. As usual, the western New York winter had been long and dreadful. Not only was the weather annoying, but emotionally I needed a lift. Terry and I were basically empty nesters and ready for a change.

Perhaps a trip to Florida would fulfill the yearning we felt in our souls. Since the boys had been little, their grandparents' small one-bedroom condo in Clearwater, Florida had often been a place of refuge and refreshment for us. In December 1995, Mother Weaver, now advanced in years, had graciously given the condo to Terry and his sister, Carol. Knowing how fond Terry was of Florida, Carol told us it could be ours and in the future we could buy her out when *one day* we sold our house and retired. Unknown to any of us, our faithful heavenly Father was again working behind the scenes to prepare a place for us.

Our trip to Florida was perfect. In May the beaches were empty and the water bath-tub warm. We returned home completely refreshed in time to collect Brian at the airport. The next day, Terry's first day back on campus, was about to completely transform our lives, but in the same instant be the answer to my fervent prayer. For two years I had sought God asking Him to give me fruit that would reproduce fruit. We lived in a Lake Erie beach community. I can remember one day seeking the Lord by the shore and as I surveyed the expanse of the jagged shoreline saying something to this effect, *"God I want fruit as the sand on the shore."* Zealous for fruit, I had repapered my kitchen walls with fruit to remind me to pray several times each day for fruit. Yes, God had been preparing my heart for a great expansion. And it, too—not unlike the shoreline—would be a jagged experience.

It was lunchtime, and Brian and I were in the kitchen surrounded by fruity wallpaper waiting for Terry to return home from his first morning back at the university. Terry joined us at the table; we prayed. I had my sandwich halfway to my mouth when he began, "I need to tell you about a notice that was in my mailbox today."

Dread entered my soul! My heart sank; I replaced the sandwich on the plate. The atmosphere was charged. What followed would change our lives forever, but not how I had anticipated. It had been a controversial year on campus, as someone had prominently displayed a pornographic art exhibit in the entrance to the library where people entering were forced to view it. In the editorial section of the college paper, Terry had taken a stand against its placement. The hot topic was polarizing to say the least, and had generated more editorial feedback than any previous article.

I awaited his news as my mind shouted to me—the dreaded pink slip! Fear paralyzed my thinking; I had forgotten that they couldn't fire a tenured professor. He began slowly; his voice was so serious. Terry proceeded to tell us that the State University System of New York was offering him an early retirement with full medical benefits for both of us for the rest of our lives. With the accumulated years he had from Cornell, Alfred, and Fredonia, he was eligible. Terry, then only fifty, had gone back to his office, gotten down on his knees, and talked to God about what had been on his heart for years—one day going to the mission field. The only obstacle that had been holding him back was health insurance for us in our retirement years. *Wow!*

That being resolved, God questioned Terry in his spirit saying, "What about now?" *Wow!*

Because we had been gone for a couple weeks, he only had days to notify them of his decision. Brian, hot off the field from his Slovakian trip, was so fired up for missions he began yelling, "Do it! Go for it! Mom, Dad, what a great opportunity!"

Without thinking, I got caught up in the excitement shrugged my shoulders and said, "Okay! Let's do it!" Little did I dream how the Holy Spirit would empower us to *do the greater things* Jesus spoke about with cutting edge ministry to unreached people groups and advancement for women in a culture where they were valued less than a cow. And that one day our lives would become a testimony of God's faithfulness to deliver His

11

kids again and again during our years in East Africa. Whether surrounded by Maasai warriors in the eerie darkness of an African night, encountering slimy snakes in the bathroom, or under siege by thieves in a remote village, over and over the Lion of the Tribe of Judah would deliver us as the roaring lion of destruction sought to devour us. God's grace carried us through years of hearing and seeing horrific things we had previously only read about—lepers with fingerless hands raised for a few shillings or the devastation of AIDS resulting in innocent orphans begging on street corners, and peril only a breath away—any time of day. Yet in all that learning to find joy in the beauty of God's creation when nothing made sense and life seemed impossibly nuts!

Terry's decision should not have come as a complete surprise to me. During the previous seven years as we leisurely walked the sidewalks of Fredonia, he would say that one day when he retired we would go to the mission field. I would just brush it off thinking—yeah, sure. I was contented with my ministry opportunities and felt fulfilled. He did not! *For the gifts and the calling of God are irrevocable.* (Romans 11:29 NKJV)

Immediately a handmade *For Sale* sign was shoved in the front lawn. Within ten days we sold our home and all our stuff. Suddenly we realized—great! We had made this awesome decision to follow the Great Commission and *go make disciples.* But what if nobody wanted us?

Because I hold credentials with Elim Fellowship, we contacted Tom Brazell, the Elim missions director, for an appointment. Determined this was the will of God for us, Terry reasoned with Tom that educational trips to the Holy Land and Greece plus seven years at Liberty University surely counted for something—even if we had not graduated from Bible college. As Terry continued, sometime in the midst of the conversation, the Spirit spoke to Tom that he should *work with these people*.

Because we had both been teachers, it was decided that filling in for a missionary teacher needing a furlough would be a good match. Finally, when Tom mentioned a place called Tanzania, I leaned over and whispered to Terry, "Where on earth is Tanzania anyway?"

He then asked Tom, "Where exactly is Tanzania?"

He replied, "East Africa."

Our problem was when we had last studied geography, it was known as Tanganyika. Tom asked if we had any more questions. "Only one," I replied, "Do they have inside bathrooms there?" His response was that, yes, they're in the missionary homes which are usually cement block with plumbing of sorts. Good thing he didn't mention the condition—if you have water.

Twenty years after surrendering our lives to Christ, we answered the call of God to go to the mission field. For the next six months we visited churches to establish relationships and gain monthly prayer and financial support. By December we had raised $1500 in monthly support and were ready to go, but for one last event—saying farewell to our sons. Christmas week Eric and Brian joined us in Tampa Bay. The final good bye literally tore my soul as they drove away for what we anticipated would be one year apart.

On January 27, 1997, Bill Clinton's second inauguration day, we left American soil for Tanzania.

Our inauguration began at Kilimanjaro International Airport (KIA). Any landing at KIA would always be the beginning of a great adventure, but our first arrival on January the 28th at about 9:30 in the evening in pitch black darkness was definitely the most extraordinary. In absolute darkness, having just skirted the highest mountain in Africa, we descended onto a runway lighted only by kerosene smudge pots. And as quickly as the plane swept by, each one was snuffed out. The excitement and anticipation was blanketed by fearful expectation of the unknown, as East Africa can be very dark and the unknown is even more intimidating. This was probably the first time I thought, *"What AM I doing here?"* Proceeding through the plane's exit door, I was overcome by the unique smell of Africa. Hot, heavy, humid air mixed with the odor of burning and sweaty, smelly perspiration immediately saturated my nostrils as I descended KLM's steps onto the tarmac.

Inside the immigration building lighted by a generator, cheerful Tanzanians dressed in brightly colored clothing greeted us with, *"Karibu. Karibuni sana!"* Karibu is the Swahili word for welcome, and they were joyfully exclaiming, *"Welcome. Welcome all very much!"* They love visitors, and most Tanzanians are eager to make new friends. Their beautiful, friendly smiles relieved the tension, and peace began to flood my soul. Waiting for us beyond Immigration was a mid-life African adventure beyond expectation.

Arusha: A Wild West Frontier Town

In 1997 Tanzania was an extremely primitive place to live. Water and electricity were semi-reliable, but often nonexistent. Our rental compound was located at the base of Mount Meru, Tanzania's second highest mountain at 14,980 feet, in a town called Arusha. Although Arusha town was a fairly large Tanzanian city of over 200,000 people, its appearance more resembled a nineteenth century Wild West town. Many local residents still grazed their goats or cows in town center. Vegetable gardens lined the sides of the road—every patch of available land was in use. From our veranda we could gaze at the majesty of the mountain as it towered over the hilly city. It was always an encouragement to me and reminded me of the scripture, *I will lift up my eyes to the hills, from whence comes my help? My help comes from the LORD, Who made heaven and earth.* (Psalm 121:1-2 NKJV) And I was truly in need of His help!

We were living together with missionaries Brick and Beth Cliff on their compound before they departed for furlough. It was part of our crash course in missions survival and a chance to get acclimated to Tanzanian culture. On the compound was a concrete house quite nice by African standards, as most Tanzanians live in mud and wood huts of various shapes. Coming onto the compound was a pipe for free flowing mountain water, which came during the night hours and was then stored beneath the ground in a carefully sealed cement cistern. During daylight hours, the outside worker would activate the pump transporting the water from the cistern to huge black plastic storage tanks placed high up on elevated cement towers. Gravity brought the *maji* (water) into the house for cooking, washing up, or bathing. No one was happy when the worker forgot to pump or when the lack of electricity prevented it! All drinking water was purified through a ceramic Katadyn filter. Boiling was only required when cholera outbreaks were in the vicinity. It was information overload!

Our garden (yard) was a place of peace and tranquility during the day. We were blessed with many flowering plants and a variety of trees, including very productive lemon and avocado ones. Growing along the perimeter of the property was a thorn hedge fence about ten feet high. In the evening three huge dogs were released to patrol the garden—one mixed breed named Carl Lewis, contributed by a departing missionary, and two fierce looking German shepherd guard dogs who understood only Swahili—one more cultural blow to my system. *Home* was a relatively safe place to be for anyone speaking Swahili!

Beth was a great hostess and prepared nutritious meals. Breakfast usually consisted of hot maize cereal called *ugi* or cold cereal topped with fresh milk or toast and eggs. Delicious fresh fruit according to season accompanied every meal. The supper meal usually consisted of game meat, either wildebeest or gazelle, with veggies and fruit. Later we added dessert, especially after I started baking for comfort food. *And I was in need of comfort!* Most of our food supplies came directly from wholesalers, so to speak. Raw milk was delivered by a neighbor. The purification process began by first straining the milk to remove bugs and animal hair. After boiling it for twenty minutes, starter would be added to about a quart of the freshly pasteurized milk to make wonderful yogurt. Later the cream which rose to the top was collected for our coffee and tea. Eggs came from another Tanzanian neighbor whose rooster doubled as the neighborhood alarm clock. Daily a banana lady arrived with an armload of various fruits for sale. Fresh veggies were obtained after bartering at the open market.

Food shopping was an aromatic experience! Our trip to the market that first week almost put me back on the plane. The smell at the Arusha marketplace was overwhelming. Rotting garbage was everywhere. Huge slabs of odiferous meat covered with flies hung on large black hooks. Those were the same flies multiplying in the *choo* (outhouse) by night. For a clean freak, it was beyond the ability to contend. In the next aisle the aroma of the barrels of *dagga,* little fish, was worse and overpowered my nostrils. *Dagga* were an excellent source of protein for the local dishes; foreigners mainly used them to mix with maize flour to concoct a filling and nutritious meal for their dogs. For white-skinned visitors, the beginning market barter prices instantly doubled or tripled. We learned early on that market shopping was better left to the household staff who loved going and chatting with all their family and friends. And they definitely got the best deals!

Our first business-type cultural experience involved setting up a bank account. Banking was always an opportunity for *shida* (problems). Simplicity does not exist in any business or government dealings in Tanzania. During the first week in Arusha, we tried unsuccessfully to open a bank account. The teller informed us we needed to have two letters of recommendation from two bank patrons. Upon returning to the bank with the two requested letters, we were further informed that we needed to bring the authors of the documents with us to get our account at the bank approved. Arrangements were made and three families met at the bank so we could have the privilege of placing our money in their bank. A year later, after returning from a furlough, Terry went to the same bank in Arusha only to be informed that the Bank of Commerce had transferred our account to another bank. And they charged us $100 dollars to do it! In 1997, that was about three months worth of Tanzanian wages. We did not handle that challenge with much joy.

The first week had definitely strained my formerly romantic ideas of living overseas for a year. But during our first worship service at the Arusha PEFA (Pentecostal Fellowship of Africa) Church, while Terry powerfully preached and monkeys plopped from treetops and romped on the tin roof, God supernaturally melted my heart with love for the people and country of Tanzania—I could feel it pouring in. On Sunday morning I was divinely grafted into Tanzania. I was smitten with a love for a wonderful culture totally beyond my wildest imagination. And it is wild—not just the wildlife, but the traditions, the fatal beliefs, the many various crises that happened daily!

As that first service progressed, a woman entered and sat in the middle of the congregation directly in front of Terry. It was extremely hot, as is usual in the months before the rainy season begins. While he was preaching, she pulled up her blouse to completely expose her chest. I was aghast; nobody else even flinched. Quickly I began to pray. Fortunately, my focused husband never even noticed her. In Africa, women commonly nurse their babies everywhere and it is no big deal. Tanzanians are typically very modest people, but in their culture it's all about covering up legs with a proper long skirt.

At the conclusion of the service we all walked outside singing the most joyous song. As they sang, they walked by and greeted everyone, and then proceeded to join the line now forming an enormous circle. The deacons then brought out all the foodstuff offerings which had been placed on the altar and put them in the middle of our circle. At the end of the singing and greeting time, an auction was held to sell off the vegetables, fruits, and other things. Everybody gave to the Lord—not out of their wealth, but out of their poverty. That day we sampled mangoes, another first and definitely a favorite! Monday we were headed to town for more of them!

Without a vehicle, Terry and I would walk to Arusha town for any necessary shopping. It was not a pleasant experience. The air was acrid with dusty billows and pungent diesel fuel from every speeding vehicle. In the months preceding the rainy season, fine powdery reddish earth collected on our feet, dusting us up to and over our ankles. That grainy red earth stained every pair of socks Terry wore with an indelible reddish orange. Even my feet absorbed the orange stain, giving a road map type appearance in the deep creases on the soles of my feet. Without a bath in bleach they never would get clean until the rains came. I hated having dirty feet all the time! The dust even layered in our ears and clogged our nostrils. We were red inside and out! When the rains came, our whole universe took a bath. Walking under a tree proved to be hazardous as all the red dust mixed with the raindrops then muddied our clothes at the top, making our outfits match our feet or our socks. Orange-red, the color of African soil, really made me appreciate normal brown dirt!

After about a ten-minute walk, we would come to the river bank. All along the bank lush, short, brilliant green grasses grew abundantly just waiting to be devoured by scores of meandering hungry Maasai cattle. The deeply gutted river bed was almost dry. Years of flood waters streaming down from Mount Meru had eroded the soil and carved deep crevices in the earth.

Gingerly crossing the river bed, skipping from stone to stone I felt like a child again back in the "cricks" of western Pennsylvania, except now I was wearing a skirt. Looking down the river bank, we were both surprised to see lush native poinsettia bushes growing wild. Brilliant red flowers topped the dusty eight to ten foot plants. Even coated with dust, they brought joy to my lonely soul; it was a happy memory of Christmas at home. As we timidly navigated the river—we hadn't quite gotten our *goat* legs yet—there was a man laughing at us from the other side. We must have looked ridiculous to him just as he looked totally bizarre to us. There he was smiling as big as a crescent moon while balancing a large cardboard box of trees upon his head. Those little tree limbs poked out in every direction creating an almost Medusa-like appearance. The more he laughed, the more menacing they appeared. Surely he must have been wondering, "*What's wrong with those Wazungu (white folks); they can't even walk right!*" We all had a great laugh as we scrutinized one another.

The river was always a busy place. Groups of brightly dressed women could be seen bent over the rocks, the local wash board, with thick yellowish bars of laundry soap in hand scrubbing the family laundry. It was then hung on the surrounding bushes or simply laid on the rocky earth to dry. It also could be an embarrassing place, as we never knew when we would come upon a naked bather. On the banks of the river Maasai guards, exhausted from patrolling compounds the evening before, often slept. One of the great conveniences of wearing a blanket as a robe is always sort of having your bed with you. They would just lie down, cover up, and sleep. They literally lay down in green pastures.

Arriving in Arusha for the first time on our own, we were jubilant feeling the power of our total independence! Moments later our pride was shattered when we discovered everything closed from 12:30 until 2 PM for lunch. In 1997 shopping opportunities in town center consisted of the Lutheran book shop, some tourist souvenir shops, and relatively few *dukas* (shops). There were three small food stores, each smaller than a typical convenience store in the States. Our favorite place of business was the Corner Grocery made famous by the John Wayne movie *Hatari* (meaning Danger). Oh, the joy of toothpaste, real Lux soap, and ketchup! In reality it was some weird, thick, red pasty sauce; we never quite appreciated it as the locals did. Prices were exorbitant, *ghali sana,* at least three times those at home, if we were fortunate enough to even find the much needed items. Our biggest disappointment—no bakery! But, the local store had some version of a stale vanilla cookie with sugar crystals sprinkled on the top tasting mildly like bug spray. Hmmm... maybe it was bug spray! By the end of the third month they tasted absolutely fantastic, and without even noticing we'd just pass the cookies! One day while in town we discovered a delicious dietary breakthrough—a newly-opened bake shop with raisin bread! As we presented the loaf to the Cliff family for dinner, our anticipation built, we were excited to try it. How we all laughed as we found FOUR raisins in the loaf—but it was indeed raisin bread, and it was delicious!

A trip to town was always an adventure. By the time we arrived home, we were literally covered with multiple layers of dust—that and whatever else lingered in the river water where the Maasai both bathed and grazed their cattle. It was definitely time for a hot bath—only to discover we had forgotten to turn on the hot water heater. Thirty minutes later we bathed! Even the bath routine was complicated. Automatically we would turn on the left faucet for that warm refreshing water to flow, experience a brief shock, and then remember again the faucets were reversed. Often we got more refreshed than we had intended! Driving, washing up, *everything* meant restructuring one's whole automatic response system, and that takes much time.

It was the simple things—like forgetting to use sterilized water that especially stressed us. Even brushing our teeth could be traumatic. Using tap water directly from the faucet could quickly infest our intestines with another case of amoeba. And adjusting to the left-right thing was a potential killer. As a former British protectorate, everything was right to left. Learning to look right instead of left to cross a street was a life-threatening challenge. I still remember the day our gardener,

Longida, suddenly flung his arm out in front of me just in time to save my life as I looked the wrong way while attempting to cross the street to the Corner Grocery. Fortunately, there were very few vehicles in the '90s due to the lack of passable roads. Trying to remember all such details contributed to the culture shock. Nothing, absolutely nothing, was normal! And there was no one with whom to register your complaints except your partner, and that could lead to both of you being depressed.

Especially frustrating to westerners attempting to adapt to Tanzanian culture is the time issue. Exact time means virtually nothing to the village people. Many city people wear watches, but for most Tanzanians not working for an *mzungu*, (white person of European descent), it's more an accessory to display wealth and position than for organizing life's schedule. In the beginning, westerners are usually more seriously enslaved to the duty of schedule. Then, after the first couple of years, they decide to relax more and live longer.

During our first year, the overseer of PEFA said that he would visit us on Monday. So Monday we remained at the compound and prepared for his visit. Three Mondays later he came. When I questioned his timing, he responded saying, "*I said I would come on Monday; I did not tell you which one.*" Oh, just another form of cultural enlightenment! Commitment to a time schedule would mean not being able to extend one's hand of friendship and greet every person (and I mean everyone) encountered on the path, from the moment leaving the home to one's point of destination and then returning home again. Hours are spent communicating this way, which is exhausting and frustrating, to say the least, to a foreigner with an *important* personal agenda. A famous Swahili proverb: "*Haraka, haraka, haina baraka!*" With hurry there is no blessing. *wow*

Greetings are a huge part of this very relational culture. One of my favorites was *salamu,* meaning peace. Early on I noticed how powerful the greeting *salamu* could be. Walking along as I greeted worried people, I noticed their countenance would often change by my just speaking a word of peace over them. But most Swahili greetings begin with *"Habari za...?"* (Meaning "what is the news of" followed by the time of day?) For example: *"Habari za asubuhi?"* (News of the morning) or *"Habari za leo?"* used later in the day, meaning news of the whole day. It would be totally rude not to speak to everyone passing by with some word of greeting. Because most everyone walks everywhere—for water, to buy or sell vegetables, plant, or harvest—traffic is heavy! Conversation could and often did fill an entire morning. Having any meeting on time was highly improbable.

Travel was arduous, as there was only one major paved road in a country the size of Texas, Oklahoma, and Nebraska combined. The tarmac went from Dar es Salaam located on the Indian Ocean westward toward Moshi, skirting Mounts Kilimanjaro and Meru to Arusha where it became what the locals called *Arusha Upper* Road. It then turned northward to Nairobi. Another main road, the *Lower Road,* leading to areas south of the Serengeti Plains and the game parks in the vicinity, was in total disrepair. Safari vehicles used to bump along the *Lower Road* at literal breakneck speed. In years past the roads had been tarmac, but by 1997 they were fractured by enormous potholes. The uneven tarmac jarred and destroyed necks and backs. Most missionaries preferred the dirt roads for the more gentle dip in and out of the ever-present gigantic potholes. Often there was more pothole than road. This was the place we thought we would call home for the next year—but Africa! Chaos and change could erupt any moment! And it did! Evicted within months by our first landlord and terrorized and threatened with death by the second—we were learning to live life on the edge!

Kigoma: A Change of Heart

After spending a few weeks in Arusha town and being totally in culture shock, Terry and I gratefully boarded a plane to travel to Kigoma. Surely this was God's gracious reprieve for us! Elim's mission strategy was for us to be acquainted with the whole nation of Tanzania, and *with pleasure*, we were leaving Arusha. We were totally fed up with all the differences and third world inconveniences such as the banking and infrequent electricity, and I just loathed the flavor of wildebeest. I was sure a great adventure was ahead!

At first our plane ride seemed fairly normal. Then off and on I kept hearing birds chirping. Later, while talking to the stewardess, I found out 500 baby chicks were on board with us. Our flight included two stopovers. First we were diverted to Mwanza to deliver the chirping chicks. Everything seemed much more peaceful after their departure. Settling back into our seats for takeoff and the remainder of our safari, we were rather startled. To our amazement, while speeding down the runway for takeoff, we passed the remains of a large old twin prop plane which had crashed. What an urgent call to prayer that was! Apparently it had been left there for years—maybe by the local evangelist.

Our second stopover was for refueling in Tabora. Everyone deplaned. All the passengers walked down the removable flight steps to relax under the shade of a tree. There everyone waited while they refueled the brilliant blue Air Tanzania plane with a huge yellow-brown giraffe painted on its tail. Under the tree we began reflecting on the craziness of the morning—birds on the plane, then the plane crash! What a reminder that the days and times of our lives are ordered of the Lord. God had gotten our attention. And He was about to correct our attitudes which were desperately in need of an adjustment. Kigoma would do that for us!

It wasn't long before Kigoma began to make Arusha seem like paradise. Kigoma is situated on the shore of Lake Tanganyika, which borders and separates Tanzania and the Democratic Republic of Congo. We left Arusha with high expectations. We were excited to be able to teach. By teaching and operating in our God-given callings, we were certain things would be more orderly and normal there. Terry was to teach Corinthians; I was scheduled to teach Hebrews.

What an unexpected journey was in store for us! A hint should have been in the prefix "ki," which means "small" in Swahili. Our purpose was to teach at the Kigoma PEFA Bible School, now referred to as Lake Tanganyika Christian College because of its close proximity to the huge lake. West across Lake Tanganyika, the Congo civil war was beginning with armed guerillas infiltrating the mountainous terrain northwest of Kigoma. Before our arrival, countless refugees from Burundi, Rwanda, and the Congo had begun pouring into Tanzania during one of Africa's most bloody times of political instability. Our first Sunday in church we heard unbelievable narratives of carnage and despair. One woman from Rwanda reported that after stepping her foot on Tanzanian soil, she began rejoicing over the safety of this place. It was then that a thief accosted her and stole all that was left of her belongings. She was left with only the clothes on her back. Every remaining thing she owned had been wrapped in a cloth tied upon her back. Now even that was gone. My selfish heart began to soften and change as the Holy Spirit reminded me once again that the secret to a contented life is a heart of gratitude. I needed to be grateful for what the Lord had provided and not be continually longing for that which I could not have. I missed my sons, but I knew where they were. I knew they were alive and safe in a land of plenty. All morning we listened to refugees' testimonies of God's divine intervention in protecting their very lives while countless others had been brutally slaughtered in the homelands. The Congo, Rwanda, Burundi—each country had a choir comprised of misplaced people with literally nothing left but their breath to praise the Lord for their lives. And they did! Radically I was moved to tears, reminded of the grace and mercy of God in my own life—to be born in the land of the free. It was definitely a moment of truth with life-changing consequences. Graciously, the Holy Spirit was breaking me again into a vessel usable for the Master's purpose. From that day forward it was not to be about me, but about Him and them.

The Kigoma PEFA Bible School was situated on the road leading to the refugee camps. On one hand there was inexpressible joy in my heart as I shared with the Bible school students. Outside, in direct contrast to the teaching of Hebrews—a book exalting the excellence of Jesus Christ, was the devastating result of man's fallen nature. Daily, truckload after truckload of civil war refugees sandwiched together passed by our classroom going to the already overloaded local refugee camps.

Three nations brought to utter destruction. A work of darkness where God's reconciling light was needed to shine brightly! Certainly those Christian college students were chosen by God *for such a time as this.* They were chosen to carry God's message of healing and deliverance to those lost, displaced souls—souls that were greatly in need of the cleansing power of the Spirit of Christ to transform hearts and bring healing and peace.

While in Kigoma, we rented a room in a large guest house on the Norwegian compound. People from all over the world lived there. Some studied butterflies and birds. Others did humanitarian medical work. We all used a communal kitchen and common bath. Daily the electricity went off from about 2-4 PM. At night the generator roared until bedtime if the national electricity ceased. Bedtime and lights out was their decision. It made for a very stressful study time as we never knew when the electricity or the generator would quit. Our daily food allotment was two eggs and some bread. We were losing much weight. I was still clueless as to how to cook without a grocery and had no knowledge of the location of the local town market. We used to say God especially provides for orphans, widows, and clueless missionaries. And He did! From the first Sunday when we met them until we left Kigoma weeks later, the wonderful Braaten family was to us an authentic example of the body of Christ in action. Daily Linda and her daughter, Candace, graciously prepared lunch for us—all totally from scratch. Hmmm ... Candace's chocolate pie! Their family lived in a single family home on our same compound. Other homes were occupied by various ministries and missionaries including a Baptist surgeon, Dr. Susan Smith, and refugee missionaries from Rwanda, who ministered to the growing number of their former church members now seeking shelter and peace in Tanzania. The compound was completely open except for a simple chain across the driveway. Anyone could walk in!

The road directly in front of the compound was the main road leading from the shore of Lake Tanganyika into Kigoma town. Periodically refugees could be seen straggling by—a further reminder of the devastation of the civil wars. Our hearts were overwhelmed by the horrors of their sufferings. God was quickly getting everyone's attention as to the need in such a place as this. Shortly after our arrival, the Kigoma PEFA church sponsored a food distribution for the refugees belonging to the Pentecostal Evangelistic Fellowship of Africa churches. We all arrived early to arrange the banquet-sized tables, formerly our classroom desks, into a U-shape and then waited to receive our instructions concerning the distribution process. As we waited, we could hear the church doors loudly rattling as bodies were thrust against them. Although the enormous wooden doors were latched with huge slide bolts, they could barely restrain the pressure from without. We could hear the moaning and clamor of desperate hearts. As the refugees pressed to enter, the Bible school students helped to maintain order and prevent a possible mob scene. Some even authoritatively stepped in front with their arms flung wide open becoming a human barricade. The desperate crowd's need was so great that those in the front were being pushed and almost crushed from behind.

Once inside, first came a sign-in and verification of PEFA church membership in Burundi, Rwanda, or the Congo; next each one got a blue plastic Marlboro bag in which to place the supplies. Then every needy saint would travel from station to station as we, PEFA missionaries, would measure out the dry goods and distribute the soap, sugar, tea, and rice. The heat of the equatorial sun beat intensely upon that corrugated tin roof as hundreds passed by feeling some of God's love lavished upon them. They were beaten down, but not forgotten as we missionaries were able to give them a cup of cold water in Jesus' name because someone in America cared enough to give sacrificially.

Afterward we all rejoiced in what those few hours had meant in the lives of our African brothers and sisters in Christ, but emotions change quickly in a culture of unknowns. Many mistakes were made innocently those first months and years for lack of knowledge. That night I learned a huge lesson. Exhausted, we each fell into our own twin bed and pulled the mosquito netting down. Hours later I was awakened suddenly by itching and the pain of being bitten as fleas swarmed all over me. Jumping inside the covers, each one was held captive by my *protective* mosquito net. Not realizing the consequence, I had parked my egg-infested shoes under my bed. Never did I do that again! I starting screaming as Terry was sleeping peacefully in the twin on the other side of the room. Eventually I crawled in bed with him as he chided me for yelling at him because I had fleas and he didn't. Lessons learned—never sleep without Doom, Tanzania's premiere bug spray, within a hand's reach. And never—no, never—put your shoes under a bed surrounded by mosquito net!

Some weeks later, as we sat on the Braatens' porch waiting for a ride to the Bible school, the US Embassy called. It had been reported to the Embassy that some soldiers with AK 47s had landed on our side of the lake. They asked Ron Braaten if his family needed to be evacuated. Then he gave a head count and hung up. Stunned, we sat on the porch hearing the words evacuation, and the number given which didn't include us! Ron certainly did not know we hadn't told the embassy our whereabouts. As he reported on the number in his family and hung up, Terry and I began shouting, "Call him back tell him there are two more." Now that will put panic in the heart of a true coward sitting about an eighth of a mile from the shoreline! Dying for the Gospel was not yet in the hearts of these two mid-life Gospel warriors. The incident was accurate, the cause misunderstood. Yes, a boatload of Congolese soldiers, who were indeed carrying AK47s, had landed on the Tanzanian shore the evening before. But, they were soldiers coming to surrender; weary men just tired of war.

There was more than one surrender beginning that day as we were learning to take up His cross daily no matter what the cost and live a life of absolute surrender amid impossible challenges. Indeed that was the spiritual lesson we were learning, but on the practical side, we needed to inform the embassy whenever we planned to change our location.

For many years a daily walk has been one of our better habits. While a graduate student at Liberty University studying Christian counseling, I gleaned the importance of daily companioning and communicating with one's spouse. Walking together with no distractions was our method for accomplishing both those goals. So even in Africa we continued to walk together and often happened upon some strange circumstances. While in Kigoma one afternoon, we ambled along finding ourselves on a peninsula in the midst of a Tanzanian army camp. There was indeed a "keep out" sign which, of course we could not read. There were no guards, for all were lounging in the shade of the trees following a big lunch. When finally they realized some unwelcome guests had strolled in, many jumped up, weapons now in hand! Arms high in the air, we quickly declared our apology and innocence. Fortunately, one of the soldiers could speak English. Once again our lives were spared from any harm. Surely they knew by looking at us we could not possibly have been spies from across the lake. War meant diligence only when it wasn't lunchtime. But seriously, because of the political unrest it was not uncommon for some of our students from other countries to be rounded up and questioned as possible camp jumpers or trouble makers from the other side of the lake. Police could readily identify tribesmen from the other countries. Immediately they came under suspicion; to the police, anyone outside of the refugee camps was suspect. Fear and anxiety filled the atmosphere.

Rookies United

Arriving back in Arusha, we were so grateful! Our attitudes were in the process of being corrected and we were excited our first term of the Moshi Bible School was soon to begin. We had surrendered to God and were ready to get involved with the community and be part of whatever the Lord had for us. Empowered by that recent act of surrender, I had walked alone to visit some friends to encourage their daughter, who had not been feeling well. That was the beginning of a God-ordained connecting thread with the Australian Rothery Family. After saying goodbye, I began my walk home along the *Upper Road*, the Arusha-Moshi Road through town. After crossing the bridge, I decided to take the shortcut home. The path wound through an uninhabited brushy area beside the tennis club ending on the road leading to our residence. The club was next to our compound.

It was a dark, cloudy, dreary day similar to all those after the long rains cease. The whole city was impatiently waiting for the sun to shine again. Without the sun to warm things during the day, homes were damp and cold. The dampness was especially felt after crawling into bed at night—it took a long time to warm those clammy sheets—and again in the morning when using a cold soggy towel to attempt to dry. We called it winter, but it was just very damp and felt chilly with temperatures ranging from the mid 50's to the low 70's. We all waited with the same impatience that everyone clamored for the rains to come after many months of heat and dust.

On my way home, I carried a satchel filled with books which were becoming heavier by the moment thus my decision to take the shortcut. I crossed the Temi River Bridge and turned onto the isolated path. As I crossed the narrow bridge, I noticed a young man glance in my direction. He then proceeded to cross the street and head toward me. The Swahili word for *help* had not yet been programmed into my brain.

I was now committed to a route which was indeed a dangerously lonely choice. Walking speedily along, I could hear his footsteps drawing closer. It was too late to turn around. The gap between us was narrowing. Louder and louder his footsteps became on the path as he swiftly closed in behind me. In terror I began to sing the chorus, "The Joy of the Lord is my Strength." As soon as I began to sing and make this confession before the Lord, around the bend came the biggest, tallest, most handsome black man I have ever seen. He was dressed in police khakis. Smiling broadly he looked straight at me and said, *"Jambo, Mama! Habari za asubuhi?"* (Hello, woman! What's the news of the morning?") How I wished I could tell him a Swahili thing or two. No need—Almighty God was in control! Still shaking but totally relieved, I found my voice and weakly replied, *"Nzuri."* Nzuri , meaning *good,* was almost always the answer even if some guy was about to knife you and take your stuff. When the no-good thief saw this huge "police officer," or rather my tall, black guardian angel, he made a wise decision to change his plans and vacate the area! *Are not all angels ministering spirits sent to serve those who will inherit salvation?* (Heb. 1:4 NIV)

Back home I quickly related to Terry my angelic encounter. There were daily reminders of God's faithfulness; truly He held our lives in His everlasting arms. *The eternal God is thy refuge, and underneath are the everlasting arms.* (Deut. 33:27 KJV) In Psalm 31:15ff, David says it like this: *My times are in your hands; deliver me from my enemies and from those who pursue me..... How great is your goodness, which you have stored up for those who fear you, which you bestow in the sight of men on those who take refuge in you. In the shelter of your presence you hide them from the intrigues of men.* If I have learned and relearned anything during the years, Father God is indeed faithful. It was the trials by fire that cemented that truth in me. Both of us continued to praise God, amazed at His grace over our lives as we continued to prepare for the upcoming Bible school term. Our excitement was overflowing! This was our purpose; our destiny was about to be fulfilled! We were soon to discover how much was involved in our new ministry besides teaching.

On opening day, our first discovery was that there was absolutely no water in the vicinity. Normally the students bathed and washed in a river that was across the road from the school. It seems this is what was meant by "running water"! Usually additional water would be carried from the river to fill a large concrete cistern on the school grounds. This year the river was completely dry; no rain had fallen for over a year in the area. While this would have been a major problem in America, life was much simpler in Africa. Eager village women were hired to carry five gallon buckets of water on their heads from a spring about one and a half miles away. That got school started. As the week continued, we shifted to men on bicycles.

39

For the same price (about 30 cents) they carried not only the five gallon bucket on the back fender, but were also able to drape two 2-gallon containers over the back fender like saddle bags. By the end of the first week we were able to hire a water truck to fill the cistern.

The next problem we encountered was the volume of dust. It had been so dry that when the wind blew, so much dust whipped through the glassless church building windows that at times we could hardly see the students in the back of the room. By the end of the day, we were all covered with a thick orange-red layer of sweat and dust. We looked just like the red stained houses we passed on the way to school. One day the wind blew so hard in the afternoon that a large box of chalk, notebooks, and even an eraser blew off the front desk! This problem was solved like many of the problems in Tanzania—we simply decided that it would not be a problem. So when the wind blew, we slammed our Bibles shut, turned our backs against it, held our breath, and grabbed everything in sight. That's just the way it was—another problem was solved!

From the beginning God blessed our time at the Bible school and knit our hearts with the hearts of the forty-three students, mostly pastors, attending our first term. One of the new students was a Maasai who shared the following testimony with the class: *"I was a member of a church and I had never heard the gospel message of salvation. But I was always feeling something lacking in my life. I had no peace at all and was restless. By chance I got a New Testament (in Maasai) and opened to Matthew 11:28. After this I felt a burden in my heart, knowing not what to do. I went to see my priest and told him about the verse and how I was feeling. Instead of helping me, he warned me not to go on reading the Bible, because if you read the Bible too much, you get confused. I left him feeling restless and more confused. One day a preacher came to our village, and I thought I would ask him about it. It was there that I got the truth, my heart bloomed, and I received Jesus as Savior. After this I used to go to the top of a hill alone to read the Bible and pray. I had read from the Bible about the Holy Spirit, but knew nothing more, only I felt excited when I read. One day I was sitting on the hill when I saw an opening in the sky, just a small inlet, and something like a spark of fire came out and landed on me. Wondering what had happened, I opened my Bible and came across Joel 2:28. When I read it, there it was. I was baptized by the Holy Spirit; for hours I was there. Another day as I was on my mountain of God I saw another vision—downhill to the east I saw a beautiful, bright, and shining city, and upon it was a white lamb, and a voice told me, go and get hold of him. I didn't know how. Another day I saw another vision from the same spot—a large multitude of people before me, and a voice said, "Go and help them. Preach to them." Although I was scared, I knew the Lord was calling me to serve Him—and that is when I started making plans to come and join the Moshi Bible School."* Brother Lukas was an example of the men and women studying at the Bible school in Moshi—hungry and desperate for more of God's Spirit!

That term Terry and I were scheduled to teach *The Shepherd and His Work*. The class was specifically designed to prepare church leaders to minister to the body of Christ. After prayer, we felt God led us to divide the course according to our personal strengths. On Tuesday morning while I was teaching

41

on the prayer of faith, the Holy Spirit directed us to begin to pray for faith to rise up in our hearts. We prayed believing for God to use us to do the greater things that Jesus spoke about in John 14:12. As we began to pray with great fervency, men began to weep before the Lord. Then God led us to pray and believe for their nation, churches, families, and ministries. God moved mightily. Prayer continued for two hours. God gave me a prophecy for them. God was lighting a fire within their hearts; they would carry it like torches to the villages, and it would spread in Tanzania. As the powerful presence of the Lord manifested, the Holy Spirit gave us scripture after scripture to be shared, other prophetic messages came forth, and finally great songs of praise. They were encouraged. For many it was the first time they had personally heard the voice of God and clear direction of the Holy Spirit. Overwhelmed by His presence, students began to dance as the glory of the Lord filled our church classroom. It was an amazingly glorious day! As for us, the Holy Spirit filled our hearts to overflowing with the joy of the Lord.

And we needed it. Homesickness was settling in and we missed our sons so much! One day during those first months in Tanzania, as I was alone in my room crying out to God, He spoke clearly to my spirit and said, "I am teaching you the suffering of loneliness." I often remember that, for it comforts me even now to remember and remind myself once again that God is involved in *my everything.* No matter what the situation, Jesus is the Director of the circumstances of my life.

One of the key factors leading to my feelings of loneliness and isolation was the surprising news that our son, Eric and

Elizabeth desired to get married. Financially there was no possible way we could return to the USA and be part of their joyous day. We released them to go ahead and marry with our blessing. We did not feel we could ask them to put their life on hold because we would be absent for a year. So on March 11, 1997, they went to the justice of the peace in Syracuse, New York and were married. On March 11 in Arusha, Tanzania I went into our garden and selected a symbolic cluster of fragrant white frangipane blossoms and some greens. With that bouquet, I celebrated their love. Ceremoniously I placed the carefully arranged bouquet on a cold faux wood and chrome table in a sparsely decorated, uninviting dining room lacking any decoration or color except for the picture of a crowned crane. Never before had I experienced such emptiness, such loneliness. I, too, felt void of life, drab, suffocated by the loneliness, and imprisoned by windows covered with bars keeping the thieves out and me in.

The date the Holy Spirit descended at the school was March 18th—also Brian's birthday! How we missed his sweet presence; the joy and laughter he brought whenever he was around. In three months we had spoken on the phone only once and that had cost us twelve dollars a minute. Seven days before, on March 11th, Eric and Liz had been married. We had only met Liz once, so we didn't even really know the one to whom our son had given his heart. We were desperate to be part of their lives. Today Elizabeth is like a daughter to us, but that period of time was one of the most difficult ever.

A few times during the decade we were in Tanzania I had those same March 1997 feelings of lonely desperation. Each time was

43

a season before God brought about a great change in my life. Truly it was a time of separation unto Himself before releasing a new season of life and ministry—bringing a break with the former things to usher in the new thing.

Behold, I will do a new thing, now it shall spring forth; shall you not know it? I will even make a road in the wilderness and rivers in the desert. (Isa. 43:19 NKJV)

We had many lessons to learn, but God had granted us an open heaven in Moshi that day. It was a new day and a new wineskin! There were new missionaries with a new vision of partnership ministry. During our class times or in church services, we made a point of speaking highly of each other. We wanted to demonstrate for them the biblical power of unity in the ministry and in the home. Because we taught the class together, the men students saw how God could use both men and women together as servant partners in ministry. Continuing in this vein, we challenged them to bring their wives in June for a marriage seminar. This would be a first. Bus fare for the women alone would be a monumental task for these men: 1000 shillings or about 1.60 US dollars per wife. We told them if they bring them here, we would give them their bus fare home. Some men made the suggestion of giving up their beds for their wives—a miracle! Then another said they could sleep on the floor of the church so the wives could come. It was becoming clear to us that one of our ministries to them was to model the power of a husband and wife in unity fulfilling the call of God together. For the first time they were catching the vision for partnership-leadership.

Feeling empowered by the morning's success, I was emboldened to relax with a stroll along the Karanga (Peanut) River a short distance from the Streets' home. During our early Arusha days, ministering in Moshi had the added pleasure of an extended visit with our special British friends, Steve and Anne Street. Their cozy house was a safe, modestly comfortable home—a place where their guests could actually drink the tap water and brush their teeth without fear of contracting amoeba. Their water source was a deep well or "borehole," as the British call it, associated with the International School of Moshi. The Streets' cottage home was a refuge for those needing a place to make a phone call, spend a night in transit from Dar, or just taking a retreat from the pressures of everyday missionary life in Tanzania.

On the rear side of the house was a steel mesh reinforced screened porch with a spectacular view of Mount Kilimanjaro. Most late afternoons included a quick glimpse of Kilimanjaro as the rain clouds covering the mountain parted just before sundown. The porch was the gathering place for the Street family and their visitors to share a cup of tea and exchange the news of the day. We met the most amazing people there from all over the world. Outside the security of the porch, Anne's garden was a delightful place filled with exotic plants the colors of God's rainbow. Located immediately inside the entrance to their home was an old fashioned dial-up, black phone equipped with a security lock-up code. Beside it on the stand lay a registration book for recording one's time and minutes of usage. Phones were a luxury back then, and Steve Street, a faculty member of the International School, was blessed to have one. They viewed every blessing as from the

Lord and were willing to share whatever they had with those without.

The river had become a familiar place where Anne and I, binoculars in hand, had previously walked together. It was serene, yet wild with massive vegetation where unusual species of birds often nested. She had taught me the joy of discovering a new variety of African bird resplendent in its variegated plumage. I remember the day I spotted one she had never seen before—that was a proud moment! The riverbed below was littered with huge volcanic boulders stripped loose from the mountainside during the torrential long rains of March and April. Streams of water would violently cascade down the sides of Mount Kilimanjaro and empty in a raging force into the Karanga riverbed.

The rains now passed, the water flowed gently, fed by the normal glacier runoff. Crossing the river was a usable but very scary looking older bridge which gave access to the coffee and banana plantations and Chagga communities settled further up the sides of Kilimanjaro.

I walked carefree down the steeply rutted dirt road and paused at the bridge to gaze at some beautiful glistening variegated sunbirds flitting among the wild trumpet plants. Trumpet plants are so powerfully fragrant, almost sickeningly sweet, that it was often said, "One trumpet plant in a garden is more than enough!" Refreshed by the beauty of God's glorious creation and the soothing music of the brook, I retraced my steps along the steep mountain road. Walking in Tanzania was not just a casual meandering. Safety required a high level of diligence. Everything from sharp objects to sunning reptiles could be found on a road. As I walked around the next bend in the road, I heard some voices. Looking up I discovered a large group of young men moving quickly toward me. Their hostile tone seemed to suggest they were irritated about something. Each carried a *panga* (machete) in his hand. The sharply-honed blades literally glistened in the bright midday sun. I was sure this was the end of me—more than just chopped liver, chopped me!

Terror immediately struck my soul! Then just as quickly my fear dissolved as each young man's face broke into a beautiful smile exposing their sparkling white teeth. Almost in unison they cried out, "Jambo, Mama," as they casually went by. Somehow I found my voice, smiled broadly, then, timidly replied, "Jambo." Thanking God over and over, I breathlessly ran back to the Streets' home, taking refuge once again on their screened porch. I was beginning to learn that Tanzanians are generally not *kali* (fierce) people, but very social and caring.

Time has changed the pristine environment along the river. It is no longer a tranquil bird sanctuary, but an industrial site of sorts. Men claim a boulder and from morning to night chip away at it. Later they sell their piles of hand hewn rocks to local construction businesses. Serenity is a thing of the past. The beauty of the wilderness is gone. It has become an industry equipped with a local gal bringing *chai* for sale. She opened a small café. Hunched down under a rectangular shaped shelter fashioned from an old maize bag which she skillfully tied to four sticks, men now find refreshment in the tea, not in the birds and babbling water. Time changes many things, but God remains the same. *I the L*ORD *do not change.* (Mal. 3:6, NIV)

Unlike the riverbed which was dramatically changing, classroom attitudes were slow to change when it came to family issues. When discussing marriage, one of the older students told Pastor Lazaro that kissing and hugging were western thoughts and that we should not allow these things to be taught! Generally women loved the marriage class but the husbands really didn't care for it. No, they hated it! Trying to teach Tanzanian Christian men, even pastors, to understand that God wanted them to love and respect their wives and not just dominate and control them was a formidable challenge. Whenever teaching on family matters, I often included this verse: *Husbands, in the same way be considerate as you live with your wives, and treat them with respect as the weaker partner and as heirs with you of the gracious gift of life, so that nothing will hinder your prayers.* (1 Peter 3:7 NIV)

Attempting to pull down generations of faulty beliefs and strongholds concerning women was the Holy Spirit's job. And truly that task was a supernatural one.

Shortly after the end of the term, the Braaten family from Kigoma contacted us with the terrific news that they were taking a safari throughout Africa and would come through Arusha on their way home. We were invited to join them on safari to the Serengeti. Miraculously God worked it out for Brian to come and join us. But not for the reason we thought— a spectacular safari highlighted by the wildebeest migration or an amazing morning when three cheetahs surround our

48

vehicle to enjoy some rest in its shade—but to plant a seed in his heart for the people of Tanzania. During his visit, Brian fell in love with the country and its diverse peoples. By the end of the first week, he was already singing in Swahili, *"Nakupenda Bwana,"* (I love you, Lord) with the compound employees. He just absorbed the language. After returning to America, it wasn't long before his missions director asked him when he was going to join his parents in Tanzania. Contacting several churches, he shared his vision and was able to raise the necessary monthly support. By the following year, Brian would be on a plane for full-time ministry in Tanzania destined for a life of great challenges but exceeding joy. While he raised funds, we continued to minister and acculturate in Tanzania.

Gospel Warriors Encounter the Maasai

In the beginning of our Tanzanian journey, the Kiswahili language was a major hurdle for us. Our language skills were basically nonexistent. Terry had taken a three-week introductory course at the Norwegian School at Usa River. The class was a very basic survival course for marketplace communication and entry level conversation with the nationals. Because we were only to be there one year and the cost was $1500, we decided I would not attend. It was my biggest missionary mistake. Language is a fundamental part of who a person is. Ability to directly communicate in a person's mother tongue is essential for heart to heart dialogue, and effective one-on-one ministry—even friendship—demands it.

To compensate for our lack of ability in the language in the early years, we would schedule showings of the *Jesus Film* in Swahili, one of the most powerful depictions of the life of Christ as recorded in the Gospel of Luke. Just getting out to the area for the presentation of the *cinema*, as the Tanzanians called it, was adventurous. Tanzania's agrarian culture and limited literacy make the film an extremely effective ministry tool. Many times during our first years, the Lord opened the way for us to participate in this evangelistic outreach. The first time was in a village located on the side of Mount Meru called *Ngare Nanyuki*, meaning red water, so named after the brownish-red bog water in the area. This was a joint effort with our Baptist missionary friends, Dr. Paul and Betty Smith. Not only were we unified in the showing, but all the local churches were united together eager for salvation to come to their region! And the enemy didn't like it. All day it had rained and the rushing mountain streams were rapidly overflowing. Oblivious to the dangers ahead, we gawked out the window as we passed giraffe after giraffe. We were thrilled; wow, what an awesome place!

Being stranded in mud was always a possibility during the rainy season, so for group safety we had decided to caravan our vehicles. We were driving our low-to-the-ground Subaru, so crossing any stream was an adventure, but that night it was necessary to cross several swollen streams to get to the village. After finally arriving, our Baptist friends turned to us saying, "We thought you didn't see the bridge in that last stream, but then you swerved at the last moment and hit the bridge by inches."

 Our response, "What bridge?" There was a five foot drop-off on both unprotected sides of the cement bridge, which was totally under rapidly rushing waters. We never saw it! Once again our prayers for guidance and protection had released God's angelic protection and the Lord had intervened and saved us for His work. Truly, *the angel of the LORD encamps all around those who* *fear Him, and delivers them.* (Psalm 34:7 NKJV)

Once there, we got stuck in the mud up to our axles—a problem to be dealt with later! Not really a problem, as there was always plenty of manpower around willing to give a helping hand. The cold mountain drizzle continued throughout the evening. It ran down the screen and over the plastic raincoat we had draped over the projector. Still the show went on. Certainly the rain did not dampen the passion of over three hundred people who stood in the chilly rain mesmerized by the story of Jesus. That night, sixty of them met Jesus for eternity. Then they gathered together and graciously pushed us and our 16 mm projector out of the mud as we carefully headed to the guest lodge on Mount Meru.

The next morning we sat among framed photo shots of John Wayne, Red Buttons, and others of the cast of *Hatari* (Danger) shot on location at the lodge. We walked to a nearby watering hole and tried to catch a glimpse of the hippo in residence. What an exciting yet scary adventure that was. I can still remember Paul walking about with knife in hand. At that point we were all still certain lions or snakes were waiting behind every bush to devour us! But the only lion seeking to devour us was the unseen enemy of souls. The darkness in that Meru region was overwhelming. Indeed our battle was not against flesh and blood, but a principality of darkness that held sway on that mountain. Continually its influence challenged our every activity. I always thought a warrior was one engaged in a battle of sorts, but Webster infers that one should also be experienced in war. We were equipped with God's armor for the battle—the experience was yet to come. Our battle was more with the invisible than the visible. And it did rage both day and night, mostly at night. When darkness falls in Africa, *darkness falls!*

After the great success with our friends, we were ready to set out on our own; we felt empowered! Again up the mountain we went, but this time in a region closer to Arusha. We took our grey Subaru station wagon and headed up the severely rutted rocky road embedded into the side of Mount Meru. It was actually more like a dry river bed than a road. Mount Meru, the continent's third largest mountain, towers over the Arusha district. The journey straight up the mountain was relatively uneventful. We left home at about four in the afternoon to give us plenty of time to arrive and set up before sundown at about 6:30.

Traveling in the daylight was definitely safer and provided an assurance (or rather the fantasy) of having some sort of control. Before long, inquisitive children began to gather. Back in the late nineties, sighting a *mzungu* was exciting and yet terrifying to these village children. They loved touching our silky hair and caressing our white skin. This was surely a conundrum, because lingering in their minds was always the family taboo—the possible danger of being eaten. Children were told by their parents that if they were not good the *mzungu* would come and eat them. So in Tanzania, we white folks had the glorious reputation of being that culture's *boogeyman*. Factor *that* into your mission statement!

On the premiere evening we began to learn one of many cultural practices among the tribes. Shortly after our arrival at the cinema site, an older church deacon with sincere good intentions picked up a switch and began wildly swinging it at the legs and arms of the little children to drive them away, as he believed them to be bothering us. Little did he know or understand God's heart's desire was to draw them to Himself even as a hen gathers her chicks. Every day, everywhere we went we were gaining insights into the depth of the need of the Holy Spirit's transforming power in the lives of the tribal people surrounding us.

After setting up the large portable screen, the archaic 16 mm reel-to-reel projector, the sound system, and making the generator hum, our African employees would begin to worship powerfully. In the quietness of a mountainside village, the sound of lively Gospel music spread for miles. People by the hundreds would begin to gather as the sun set and music filled the air. They loved seeing the cinema about a God who could surely identify with them. After all, Jesus walked dusty roads. And the people in the cinema planted and harvested much the same as those in rural Tanzania do even today. After the completion of the *Jesus Film*, Terry would get with a translator to share the Good News that God's message of love and salvation is for all of them regardless of tribe, gender, or age. Eagerly many would then respond to God's message of hope for eternal life.

The region around Arusha is predominantly inhabited by the Wameru, the people of Mount Meru, and a Maasai tribe called the Warusha, or people of Arusha. About every five years, the Maasai have a season of warrior initiation. For the local Maasai tribe, this took place somewhere on Mount Meru during our first year in Tanzania. The young men from about the age of 13-18 were taken from their families and moved away from the rest of the tribe. There the elders trained them in the ways of the Maasai. During this time the young initiates were dressed in plain black robes with faces decorated with white paint forming hideous, diabolical designs. The end results were terrifying. All this was done to participate in an inhumane circumcision in order to earn the right to wear the honored red warrior robes of male authority.

That memorable night we were joyfully returning home from Mount Meru, praising God for such a great Kingdom victory because many of the Wameru people had given their hearts to Jesus. Suddenly, as we bounced over a steep crest in the road, we discovered that as we traveled down the mountainside, simultaneously the Maasai warriors, en masse with their teenage initiates, were coming up to continue their initiation drills. Instantly, our joy turned to fear! They were chanting in full voice in a powerful, dreadful-sounding synchronized cadence while running up the mountain. And we were returning home in our very short Subaru station wagon. There is no darkness on earth as the darkness of a culture called the Dark Continent—with the added effect of no electricity, not a star in the sky, and, therefore, no light anywhere.

That was, except for two very small headlights encrusted with grime. Coming down the steep, rocky mountainside were two tired but excited missionaries in the aftermath of their first solo village ministry. Into our headlights came what seemed like an endless stream of red-robed Maasai along with their black-robed, evil-looking, white face-painted initiates. Each one had a spear pointed at about a forty-five degree angle, and an eighteen inch double-edged sword sticking out from under his belt. With shields raised, they came at us creating the most horrifying appearance, looking like red ants from hell.

Terror of heart set in. I was sure we were about to be lunchmeat and imminently heaven-bound. Not losing one beat, those warriors split down the center. Amazingly, our little Subaru passed directly through the middle without a scratch. Our eyes were wide open in terror and unbelief at the grace of our God upon our lives. I knew then exactly how the children of Israel felt as they passed through the waters of the Red Sea.

Fear not, for I have redeemed you; I have called you by your name; you are Mine. When you pass through the waters, I will be with you; and through the rivers, they shall not overflow you. When you walk through the fire, you shall not be burned, nor shall the flame scorch you. For I am the LORD your God, the Holy One of Israel, your Savior. (Isa. 43:1-3 NKJV)

Later as we were finally able to process the event, we realized the Lord had allowed the encounter to dramatically arouse our attention concerning His desire for the Maasai to know Him. God expanded our hearts—a passion for the souls of the Maasai tribe was ignited within us. Evangelistic fire burned in our hearts. Eternal life was at stake!

With eternity ever in mind, we were excited to be invited to show the *Jesus Film* in the Lutheran church at Iboru on the side of Mount Meru, where we had a very fiery event. Many local people, pastors, bishops, and other denominational leaders were present. We loved the freedom we experienced as missionaries to cross denominational lines and be a blessing to all the saints. I especially loved being present that evening at the Lutheran church, for it was in my home Lutheran church that I had received the heart for missions work and—most importantly—there I met Jesus. It seemed a fulfillment of destiny of sorts. The year was 1997 and our rickety 16 mm projector was still cooperating, although after almost every viewing some minor repair was necessary. It was a wonderful night as we were all nestled inside a large church with actual benches to sit on. So moved were the people by the story of Christ's miracles and His miraculous love that they watched intently. Bishops had tears in their eyes as they viewed for the first time the passion of their Lord, whom they so dearly loved. Everything was going great. That is until the image of Jesus, projected larger than life over their heads, began to burn. Jesus was burning on the cross! The projector had frozen at that precise moment. The celluloid film melted and fire spread over the Savior.

We panicked at the heresy that could have been birthed in the tender hearts of those present in that sacred place. Terror and unbelief were reflected in their eyes. What they must have been thinking! Who were these heretics anyway? When people have no knowledge of the mechanical operation of things, suspicion and fear rule and can supersede rational thinking. Frantically, Terry jumped up and turned off the projector. Then desperately he plunged into an explanation that Jesus did not really burn on the stake! It was just the malfunctioning of an ancient projector. And that yes, it is true that Jesus really did die on the cross for their sins, but He is alive today as their resurrected Lord. The anointing of the Holy Spirit was so powerful—the bishop wept and sixty people received Jesus as Savior. They left rejoicing as new creatures in Christ, changed by the power of the Gospel message burned into their hearts.

Therefore, if anyone is in Christ, he is a new creation; old things have passed away; behold, all things have become new. (2 Cor. 5:17 NKJV)

Another fiery event happened on the 4th of July when we again travelled far up Mount Meru to show the cinema. We were positioned in a field with gently sloping hillsides surrounding us on three sides, looking much like a naturally formed amphitheater. Under the vast starlit sky, we showed the *Jesus Film* to 1800 to 2000 people. Most stood for three hours, immobilized by the powerful drama before their eyes. Others climbed trees for a better view, reminding us of Zacchaeus. With all those hundreds of people pouring in, Terry carefully checked the equipment. Seconds later our huge speaker blew out—smoke was rising from it. The projector had a very small amplifier with it. He came to the car devastated; we prayed, "Only You can do this Lord. Help us let everyone hear the Gospel message." Not only did they hear, but 600 adults received Jesus as Savior that night!

We were overwhelmed with joy of what was happening on the mountain, but the enemy was not. Before long he attempted to challenge our ministry in two different ways. In many areas the Arumeru region, comprised of Arusha and Mount Meru, was shrouded with false religion. Our *Jesus Film* ministry was battling a strong religious spirit. Some very religious people, while thinking they had the whole truth, tried desperately to hinder the work of the Lord. When the cinema was coming to a specific area, the regional church "evangelist" would go around and visit the people in their homes. He would tell them it was permissible to attend the cinema, but that they didn't need to be saved. After all, hadn't they been baptized as infants; hadn't that settled the issue once and for all? At one particular viewing, many precious people raised their hands to receive Jesus as Savior. But out of fear of the religious leaders, when the invitation was given to come forward for the salvation prayer only eight came. Others seeking salvation were observed, some being physically restrained by religious zealots in the crowd. Maybe they were forbidden to follow Jesus physically—but surely no one could stop their seeking hearts. *And you will seek Me and find Me, when you search for Me with all your heart. I will be found by you, says the LORD.* (Jer. 29:13-14 NKJV) Truly God sees the seeking heart.

The second diabolical attempt to thwart what God was doing occurred late one night as we traveled home from another showing on the mountain. The night was intensely dark. No electricity was in the area and even money for kerosene lamp oil was scarce. Starving people don't spend money on such luxuries as kerosene, soap, or toilet paper. As we came over a rise in the road, our headlights fell upon a woman lying on the side of the road. Our initial response was to be *Good Samaritans* by stopping to render assistance. But as soon as Terry began braking, the Holy Spirit checked him. Instantly he knew—danger! At the same time God quickened to me. "Drive on!" I shouted. Looking into the rear view mirror, Terry saw several hard-looking, disappointed men coming out of the bush. In the road they now stood, weapons in hand, their plans foiled by the Holy Spirit. The woman got up and walked away. Quickly God was reinforcing His principle of instant obedience to His divine guidance!

He who dwells in the secret place of the Most High shall abide under the shadow of the Almighty. I will say of the LORD, "He is my refuge and my fortress; My God, in Him I will trust." Surely

He shall deliver you from the snare of the fowler. (Psalm 91:1-3 NKJV)

Another new cinema adventure was about to open up. Directly across the tarmac which skirted Mount Kilimanjaro and Mount Meru, the savanna grasslands spread out for vast regions before being hedged by the distant Blue Mountains, barely visible on the horizon. Dotting the bush were small shrubs, tufts of grasses, isolated trees, and some round Maasai huts. Typically the Maasai live in a small village called a *boma* (compound). An individual family unit and at times extended families live on the compound. A *boma* consists of a collection of circular huts framed by sticks tied together, which are then covered by a mixture of grass, mud, and cow manure to comprise the walls, and topped by a grass roof. Sometimes at the center of the roof is a smoke ventilation hole. The huts are arranged in a circle with each hut belonging to a different wife. Encircling the huts is a thick, high wall of thorn bushes providing protection from marauding predators. Most evenings the cows and goats are also corralled in that protected area unless they are on safari for drinking water. In Maasai land, herds of cattle and goats are always on the move either going to or from the watering hole. Massive numbers of hooves stomping along the dry barren land and the winds that cut across the plains fill the air with clouds of gritty red dust. Alongside the animals, young shepherd boys clothed in red robes tied at one shoulder walk with their muscular, bare, dark-skinned bottoms exposed by the wind, as they brutally drive the helpless animals with sticks—sometimes beating them severely. Those animals are a sign of wealth and even prestige, but there is no conscious concern for their pain.

Coming from Arusha, we drove along the tarmac until our guide suddenly told us to turn. The grass had been chomped almost to oblivion by grazing herds of skinny Maasai goats and cattle. Bush travel was predominately by foot or bicycle on paths that were never straight. Trying to find one's way into the bush for ministry in a car during daylight with a guide was difficult; emerging from the bush when the *Jesus Film* was over was much more challenging. The guide, who was now at his *boma*, would remain with his family. Trying to navigate on goat paths to find our way back to the one main road in complete darkness was more than a little tense!

The enthusiasm and pageantry of Maasai showings made it all worthwhile. As soon as the Gospel music began, robust singing and leaping would break forth. Maasai tradition includes massive tribal jumping in unison to the beat of the music. The men dressed in red plaid robes and their wives dressed in bright blue plaid ones jumped for joy, robes and body parts flapping in the wind. One evening, as the people began to joyfully celebrate and dance, a cobra raised its deadly head, spreading its hood trying to intimidate and inhibit the worship. The Maasai warriors circled the snake and whacked it to death with the long slender sticks they typically carry everywhere. Now I knew why; I always thought they were just for leaning upon. Maasai men spend a lot of life leaning on sticks and talking. Meanwhile, Maasai women seem to do all the work such as carrying the water (some walk as far as half a day to get it); gathering the fire wood; cooking; building the house; milking the cows; going to market; caring for the children; and whatever other household duties needed to be done. They seem to do everything except shepherd the goats and cattle.

It was a wonderful evening, but although the Maasai men attended, most were not interested in Christ's free gift of salvation. Their wives and daughters ran to receive Him. This was a hard lesson to learn. Maasai culture demanded that the elders hear the message first to discuss it and then make a collective decision—thumbs up or down for Jesus. A decade later, the wisdom gained at this night's cinema would guide Terry to successfully evangelize the unreached Barbaiq tribe.

In only nine months of outreach, the *Jesus Film* was shown to nearly 13,000 people and 1,962 received Christ as Savior. God promises His Word is more powerful than a two-edged sword, accomplishing His divine purposes—never returning void!

Mosi-oa-Tunya: the Smoke That Thunders

Having received a one year (Short Term Enlistment Program) appointment from Elim, we were anticipating one year on African soil. The Bible school term ended in June and, assuming we would never have another opportunity, we decided to travel by train to Victoria Falls to celebrate our thirty-first wedding anniversary. July is usually a rather cool, slightly overcast month following the end to the rainy season. Sharing our excitement about our impending adventure with friends at the Arusha Community Church, we were surprised to hear absolutely everyone warning us not to do it! When we declared we would be just fine, they encouraged us to take lots of water along and keep our windows closed at every train station. It was customary for thieves to linger along the roadways or tracks just waiting for an opportunity to grab anything through an open window. In plain sight, they would then celebrate their victory shouting, dancing, and displaying the falsely obtained treasure before all their comrades. Meanwhile the captive passenger, fearful of losing his seat and other belongings, watched helplessly from the bus or train after closing the window.

Our journey began by Terry going into town to purchase bus tickets for the ride to the "unofficial official" capital of Tanzania, Dar es Salaam. The actual capital is desolate Dodoma, but public officials refused to move there, so all the government offices remained in Dar except Parliament, whose members commute back and forth. The bus trip to Dar should have been a clue as to what was ahead. Since it was our anniversary, Terry lovingly tried to surprise me by purchasing the high priced deluxe bus tickets. Naturally, we anticipated a ride equivalent to the description. Hidden in the enticing word "deluxe" was the promise of a semi-chilled Coke. East African buses are typically staffed by a driver and a barker, who screams loudly to encourage potential passengers to engage their bus. Our deluxe full-sized coach had an additional employee—a hostess. The trip was advertised to be a direct nonstop route to Dar. That is a very important detail, as it is essential to arrive and be settled into one's hotel before dark. Our seats were covered with a rough velour-type material brightly decorated with a red, orange, and yellow scrolled pattern. They were fairly comfortable and even reclined slightly for the trusting individual who chose to close his eyes. So we settled in for the ride. But this "direct" bus stopped at every single little dirt road junction from Arusha to the outskirts of Moshi—a distance of about 60K adding an extra hour and a half onto the normal eight-hour trip abounding with some horrific road conditions.

After leaving the populated areas, the barker retrieved a newspaper from the cupboard above the seats where all important personal valuables were stowed. He opened it, spread it carefully on the floor, promptly layed down on it and proceeded to take a nap in the front mid-section of the aisle. Three-fourths of the passengers were behind him, but the hostess and the cooler with the Cokes were in the front row. Once we entered the nomadic bush region, she began to pass out the Cokes. In order to pass out the sodas to the rear passengers located behind the barker, she had to step over his head by carefully placing one foot by his neck and shoulder and then the other one between his legs. She repeated this until everyone was served. And the bus was full.

Now in my western way of thinking, I could not imagine why she did not just awaken him and tell him to move while she served the passengers. As I sat there contemplating this male-female indignity for about thirty minutes, suddenly the bus driver slammed on the brakes, pulled over to the side of the road and abruptly stopped our deluxe coach. Every male passenger disembarked, took a wide upside down v-shaped stance on the left side of the bus, with his back to us, and proceeded to empty his bladder. All the women exited around to the rear of the bus. I sat stunned and finally found someone who spoke English who informed me this was it! If I needed to go potty, I had better join the throng at the rear of the bus *sasa hivi!* (right now). Leaving the bus, I proceeded to its rear to find every woman there with her legs spread and the tarmac road very WET. It was hopeless, as hard as I tried, I just couldn't do this—I and my bladder froze. Suddenly I saw another *mzungu* take off into the bush. What a brilliant idea! I dropped my jumper skirt and took off after her to hide behind another bush. Unfortunately I was wearing a loose knit sweater vest, a gift from our son Brian's mission trip to South Africa, and it got caught in the infamous "wait-a-bit bush." The bush is named for its tendency to hold captive anyone coming close to its barbed thorns. Everyone was reentering the bus and I was still "waiting a bit" trying to disengage the tree. I couldn't leave Brian's gift attached to it. Oh the dilemma—and then I really felt the urgency to go! Untangling myself, I quickly pulled up my jumper skirt. Unfortunately I formed a bowl with it and collected every drop of bodily processed Coke possible.

Dropping the rather full skirt, now a reservoir for urine, my socks turned yellow and my moist sneakers became squeakers. Moving carefully and as quickly as possible, I noisily reentered the bus, relieved but definitely wet and smelly. Removing my shoes, I threw my socks out the window and then began to hang the full skirt out the window to dry. Sometime later Terry turned to me and casually commented, "Something smells." Still extremely irritated, I told him, "Just shut up!"

 By the time we reached Dar I was dry. But arriving after dark was another soon to be dealt with concern—all the unknowns, including our continual Swahili language deficiency, were more than a bit unnerving. Somehow we found a hotel and settled in for the night. I was amazed at how this very fine hotel in the "capital" was so dirty. Inches of dust collected everywhere. The electricity was off, so the city of several million had been without water for three days. Living with dust is difficult at first, but life without water is wretched. I was so grateful to God for a cold shower that extra smelly African day. We fell into bed after setting the alarm for eight. We had decided we would go to the Zambian Embassy to get our passports stamped at about ten since the train didn't leave until later in the afternoon. When I awoke at eight, Terry was already up. He felt compelled to go to the embassy right then. Arriving by nine at the gate, the guard at the door allowed Terry and two others to enter. They absolutely shut down passport applications by 9:30 AM. Many others planning to take the three-day train ride were denied service. How the Lord had blessed us by awakening Terry early with an urgency to go right then! We returned in the afternoon to collect our newly-stamped passports. Taking our seasoned African friends' advice, we stocked up on food and water. Then arriving at the train station, we found that they wanted us in separate compartments—one for men and the other for women. Telling the train manager that it was our anniversary, he did some rearranging and gave us permission to stay together along with another couple who were also traveling together. Africans are very relational and always try their level best to accommodate a guest.

Our compartment was about eight by eight with two bright orange plastic bunks stacked on each side. A table stood at the end by the window and a shelf above the bunks was for our luggage. All day and night curious people kept passing by and gawking at us. Actually some were taking stock as Terry had placed his leather hiking shoes just inside the doorway. Realizing our mistake, we moved them under the bed hidden from those searching eyes. Sometime later during the night a thief stuck his hand in the door and tried to steal the shoes. Hey, we were seasoned missionaries by now! Yeah, right! Knowing the danger of an unlocked door in a culture where anything belonging to an *mzungu* is fair game, Terry had secured the door with his leather belt. Following that excitement, it took some time to adjust to the constant swaying motion and the clickety-clack of the wheels along the track. After a couple of hours, we eventually fell fast asleep.

As we traveled south through the Mikomazi Game Reserve during the wee hours of the morning, the train came to a sudden halt. Screech! Slam! Crash! Bang! Terry flew off his bunk. We all feared the cause of the emergency. Were soldiers out there with AK47s waiting to rob us? Bewildered, we sat there for about three hours. Only later did we discover the cause—our train had hit a buffalo. He lay dead across the tracks and no one would go out to move the carcass and for good reason. The week before one of the train's employees had confronted an angry elephant lingering on the track and had been gored by his tusk. Confronting *kali* (fierce) wildlife in the middle of the night is a hazardous occupation. There is a reason they are called wild! Elephants fear nothing, not even lions. That was day two of the journey, with much more excitement to come.

One reason we were so excited to travel by train was that we were certain it would be a wonderful time of game viewing as we travelled along through the bush. We saw a grand total of one monkey and one deer critter, which was most likely an impala. Local lore has it that the country of Zambia had a horrible problem with tsetse flies, the carriers of sleeping sickness. To solve the problem a government official exterminated all the large game animals, thinking to eliminate the disease. Sadly the game was gone, but of course the tsetse flies were adaptable and merely took up residence in the smaller game animals. It seemed that daily, whether at home or on safari, we were inundated with the strange news of one sort of tragedy or another.

On the second day there was actually water for showering. The toilet was a hole opening onto the tracks. I remember the boards were decayed, wobbly, and warped. It gave me a rather suspenseful feeling while using this *choo*. I wondered if I, too, would any moment be on the tracks. Before long the community water was gone. No shower for Terry. Our first class compartment was located between the second and third class cars and the bar car. Therefore, anyone going to the bar passed by everyone seated in the first class compartments. Unfortunately many of those visiting the bar car drank too much. My getting to the bathroom became a game of tiptoe not unlike that of the Coke server girl on the bus. Drunks were sprawled everywhere. Although I wanted Terry to go with me to the bathroom for protection (I had not yet learned how gentle to their face Tanzanians are to guests), that would be impossible, for when we returned our whole compartment would have been empty. Later that day the young couple sharing our compartment disembarked. About one in the morning, the train pulled into another station. A huge Zambian woman was returning from somewhere in Europe with more luggage than our compartment could accommodate. On top of that, she tried to sneak all her third class family members into the unit. It was a common African way of economizing family transport: buy one first class ticket, then smuggle all the relatives into the prospective cabin. By the end of the day we were getting a little edgy. We put a quick stop to that and drew the line. We claimed our territory and we were not relinquishing an inch of our space! We were getting *kali* (fierce)! Space is a conceptual problem in cultural adaptation for westerners. Africans think the more the merrier, no matter how small the space, whether it be on a mini bus or a train. Their motto is, "There's always room for one more!"

Three days after leaving Dar, we arrived at the end of the line in Lusaka, Zambia. Colorfully decorated mini buses were parked close by waiting to take the disembarking passengers to Lusaka hotels. Some buses had fancy western names such as

Cold Stone or *Hillary*. Sound systems were blaring at full volume, each with a different song. The noise was deafening. The bus barkers began working the crowd, each doing his level best to coax the passengers by declaring his ride's advantage over the others. Those train passengers who tarried inside and didn't get an immediate seat on the buses were herded back into the train for one more night of waterless starvation. Things just closed down after sundown. Dark is time for locals to head for the safety of home and some warm *ugali* and *supu* (a maize dish with a vegetable soup covering). The buses dropped all the passengers at the city center bus stage. We were once again on our own. Fear gripped my heart! God faithfully intervened again for out of nowhere we met another English-speaking missionary, who was familiar with the town and invited us to share a cab with her. She directed us to an excellent hotel where we felt very safe—that is, until we got off the elevator to find a guard facing us with an AK47 pointed in our direction. Comfortable feelings are fleeting things in third world countries. Included in the hotel room literature was a warning to all visitors. *Do not purchase any gems from the local street vendors. You might have noticed there is no colored glass in our stoplights. Rubies, emeralds, and topaz are all readily available and all worthless.* Guess where the stoplights went?

The next day, we traveled by another large coach to Livingstone where we engaged a taxi to Victoria Falls. Finally arriving at the hotel, Terry inquired about the room rate which was $200 US per night. Shocked, he told them we were missionaries from Tanzania, and then he announced that there was no way we could pay that amount and that we had just traveled three horrific days to get here. Then the barter began and two more times the hotel attendant mentioned amounts of over $100, to which Terry again said, "Impossible!" Eventually the frustrated clerk asked, "Well, what can you pay?" They came to an agreement well under $100; we paid $40 and we were in. Learning to barter was a great skill to be mastered. What an anniversary gift from God—a four star hotel located on the Zambian Falls park property! Inside a sign warned us: *Do not drink the faucet water and be careful while showering not to swallow any water. Your (brown flowing) water comes directly from the Zambezi River.* Coming out of the bathroom, feeling a little squeamish, my mood brightened immediately, for right outside our door monkeys were playing in the lush green garden. They were just waiting for our garden door to be opened—an obvious opportunity to enter and steal something to playfully enjoy.

Tea time happens twice daily in former British colonies and those fun loving little thieves were especially fond of shiny metal sugar bowls. They loved the delicious sugary substance inside and something fun and shiny to play with later. In the beginning we westerners all think they are so adorable, but eventually most people consider them a menace. We, on the other hand, loved the monkeys—baboons were our trouble makers!

The Zambezi River is the source of Victoria Falls, created as they suddenly drop 360 feet off the escarpment, plunging into the river bed below. The falls are the highest in Africa. David Livingstone, the famous Scottish missionary and explorer, named them for his sovereign, Queen Victoria. The locals call the thunderous falls, Mosi-oa-Tunya, meaning *smoke that thunders.*

Further down river, the Zambezi was inhabited by hippos and crocs. On the eve of our anniversary we took a sunset cruise down the exotic river. Elephant families plunged into the water and began to swim to an island not far away. Soon all that was visible of them were their trunks as they went snorkeling by. Hippos were gathered further down river. Although awesome to behold, hippos were an animal to be feared as they can be aggressive and will flip a boat or boldly attack someone while bathing or doing the family laundry on the shore. Hippos killed more people than lions ever did. Although the multitudes of hippos did not attack our boat, they surely displayed lots of teeth and huge tusks trying to intimidate us. Much later, in the twilight, we saw silhouetted giraffes cautiously, gracefully, slowly separating their legs into position to be able to lower their long necks to be refreshed by the rapidly flowing water. Being at Victoria Falls was an extraordinary adventure. Hiking the massive falls lining the border between Zambia and Zimbabwe, we were amazed by the beauty and enormity of it all and the freedom of movement for visitors to get so dangerously close to the edge.

The falls were a true vacation site. In the rushing water people surfed the swirling pools and ran the rapids on rubber rafts; others, opting for thrills on dry land, dropped by bungee cords from the bridge joining the two countries. Some fell face first and turned stark white as they twirled and dangled head down over the Zambezi River.

In the evening, while hiking the area below the falls, I stepped into an elephant footprint. At first I didn't even realize where I was standing, until I noticed the familiar curved four-toe shape surrounding my foot. Huge! It was an amazing moment as I began to absorb the largeness of their being. The next day, as we were walking in Zimbabwe, an elephant attacked a car on the other side of the road from where we were walking. The car and its passengers were literally shaking as we carefully scooted away backwards, never taking our eyes off him! There is nothing more *kali* (fierce) than a lone male elephant in musth.

It was an awesome adventure, but when it came time to return to Tanzania, remembering the train, the drunks and the thieves, and the bus rides, I said to Terry, "If you really want to celebrate our thirty-second year of marriage, you WILL fly me home!" Did I really now call Tanzania "home"?

The Lion of the Tribe of Judah

Following our return from the safari to Victoria Falls, restlessness descended upon me. Where formerly total peace concerning our circumstances had reigned, now I felt uncomfortable in the decisions we had made.

About three days after our return from Victoria Falls, Terry came out of the office looking very serious and said, "We need to talk!" He, too, had been having thoughts like, "*What have we done?*" Only his concern was bigger; he had resigned his well-paying faculty position. Our present income was now about twenty percent of what it had been. It was barely enough to cover our local ministry and living expenses, but what about the future? Realizing we were both experiencing unrest, we knew God must be up to something. *yes –*

We decided to fast and pray for three days. Surely, God would speak to us. We definitely needed clarity and confirmation that we were indeed in His will. The decision was made to fast everything but water, and to break the fast at sundown on the third day. During the third day, Terry came and told me to pack a picnic. Our plan was to drive up Mount Meru into the forest to watch the black and white bushy-tailed colobus monkeys. We loved seeing wild game and the lush greenery on the mountainside. The clean fresh forest refreshed our souls. Later, as we returned down the mountain, we would break our fast at sundown close by a watering hole located in an area known as the Little Serengeti Plain, where the park game gathered for their last refreshing drink of the evening from the cool mountain waters.

The drive up the mountain was uneventful. At the top we delighted in the antics of the colobus monkeys chirping and jumping with white tails flopping in the breeze. On the way down the mountain we would always pass herds of giraffes, as Mount Meru is recorded as having the greatest population density of giraffes in the world. One day while on the way to show the *Jesus Film* we passed sixty-three giraffes munching the copious treetops of the surrounding hillsides. Tall necks stretched over slender branches, angling to get the tender green shoots from among thorny limbs of acacia trees. What amazing prickly black tongues they have! On occasion we would spot a timid red duiker antelope standing almost invisible in the thick brush. Coming out of the forest, often we would startle the warthogs grazing along the side of the road; they would then trot off, tails thrust straight up in the air—full of attitude. That road is now closed except for paying tourists, but in 1997 we had the freedom to bump along the jagged mountainous road whenever we wished to partake of God's glorious creation. As we slowly continued our descent, we began to talk about how sad that there were no longer predators in this park. Coming around a bend we stopped suddenly as a huge baboon was sitting in the middle of the road. As I was gazing at it, Terry exclaimed, "There goes a huge black mane lion!"

My first thought was—boy he must be hungry! Then I said, "Terry it's a baboon!" Again he said, "No, I saw a lion!" And as we proceeded around the next bend, out of the bush strolled the most beautiful lion we have ever seen, even to this day. He was perfect; there were no ticks, no scratches or claw marks on him. His thick black mane looked as if he had just left a beauty salon; every hair was perfectly in place. The lion began to amble on the road in front of us. For some unknown reason, I said, "Let's time him and see how long he walks in front of us." We followed slowly and cautiously behind him. First the lion went to the left side of the road marking it with his scent, and then to the right side of the road marking it. He did this repeatedly as we continued behind him. From time to time he would turn his huge head around and look back at us with those piercing yellow eyes. That put a tremor in my being! I was really hoping we were not annoying him too badly. For seven minutes we timed him as he continued along marking his trail. Left and then right, over and over again, back and forth he went. At the end of seven minutes, he disappeared into the bush never to be seen by us again.

Wow, we were so blessed! Our hearts were beating like crazy with excitement from what had just transpired. We couldn't believe our eyes—a lion walked in front of us for seven minutes. As we continued down the road, a family of zebras, *punda milia*, meaning striped donkeys, passed in front of us on their way for a drink. Reaching the Little Serengeti Plain, we pulled off to the side of the road elated by our good fortune of seeing the lion, but bummed out that God had not yet spoken to us! How like Africa—euphoria one moment, and the depths of despair and disappointment the next! This is one of the foremost places in the Arusha region where on a clear day in the early evening a spectacular view of Mount Kilimanjaro can be seen as the sun shone on the glacier. That day the setting sun was casting a beautiful pinkish-red hue on the mountain. Framed between Mount Meru on the left and Mount Kilimanjaro on the right were an abundance of grazing African wildlife, preparing for another possibly hostile night in the bush and us waiting to hear from the Lord.

Sundown comes around 6:30 PM, give or take fifteen minutes, throughout the year. It was getting late. Quickly we ate our homemade meatloaf sandwiches, wanting to return to the compound before absolute impenetrable darkness. It was always rather frightening driving at night. Without streetlights or any other illumination, Tanzanian pedestrians were just not visible with their backs to us. We were grateful when reflectors finally started being put on sneakers and bicycles. Arriving home, we were still disappointed that God hadn't answered our prayers. After reading for a bit, we retired early, exhausted from the day's events. We remained bewildered as to why Father God had not spoken to us.

In scripture, one of the references to the Holy Spirit has to do with water. Often when I am around water, God's Spirit will speak to me. That next morning I was in the kitchen prepping for the day when all of a sudden the Holy Spirit began to fill my heart with the following message: *"You were fasting and praying and who showed up but the Lion of the tribe of Judah saying, 'Don't go to the left and don't go to the right, but follow Me and I will lead you all the way.'"*

On August 11, 1997 at 6 PM we received an email from the former PEFA missionary in Tanzania stating that he and his family would not be returning to Tanzania. On the 11th of August 1997 the Lion of the tribe of Judah spoke to us following a fast, and then followed it up with an email—God is always on time. That was surely the confirmation we sought.

Indeed we were on a path following the Lion of the Tribe of Judah. Life as we knew it would never be the same again.

Mountain Mama

After receiving the exciting news that God's plan for Tanzania included us, we realized the financial responsibility of not only our living expenses but now also the overall costs of the Bible school would rest solely upon our own personal missions support. Excited yet stunned, confident yet scared, and definitely overwhelmed, we knew we needed to prayerfully execute a plan to make all that possible. Up to that point, our only financial responsibility was personal living and ministry expenses. Quickly our plans were propelled into action by the rapid appearance of Mama Stella, the compound owner. Within twenty-four hours of hearing the news that the Cliffs were not returning, Mama Stella stood at our gate wanting to talk. We always marveled at the speed of communication. Back in the 90's not one cell phone and very few land lines were in existence.

Upon her arrival, our landlady announced she was raising the rent by several hundred dollars. We were devastated. Within twenty-four hours time we were flying high with the news that we were catapulted into being potential career missionaries only to find out we were essentially about to be homeless. Still in shock, we offered her the customary cup of tea.

But the Holy Spirit was at work. Suddenly, Mama Stella was transformed! Her firm, businesslike nature dissolved and compassion overtook her heart. Mama Stella said, "Do you have any furniture?" "No," I replied, "we don't have anything." So she lent us the living room couch, the most coveted sofa in the region. It was not the typical African six-cushion, three squares up and three squares down, torturous wooden piece of furniture, but a real western sofa! A person could actually sit or lie down and find comfort enough to take a snooze. Next she asked, "Do you have a stove or pots or pans?" Again I responded with the same line, "We don't have anything."

She instructed us to come to her home on Mount Kilimanjaro in Marangu. Mama Stella was a Chagga princess. Her father had been the wealthy Chagga chief over the Kilimanjaro region. He had over fifty wives and hundreds of children. As a member in the local Lutheran church, Mama Stella was very respectful of missionaries, although at that point she had not had a personal encounter with Jesus the Christ. But He was at work!

Our first journey up the mountain that August 1997 day was a very bumpy experience in our low-to-the ground Subaru station wagon. Round and round the jagged mountain we drove, edging our way to the hotel owned by her brother. Any mistake could be disastrous, plunging us straight down into the ravine. Arriving at the enormous hotel, we could tell it had been grand in its day. The air was cool and refreshing; the gardens were expansive with brilliant red and yellow variegated canna lilies and various colorful groundcovers nourished by mountain mists. Travelling without air conditioning, our first request would be for the washroom or *choo* and hopefully some water for a good wash-up to remove the dirt from our faces. Looking at the beautiful structure around us, it seemed a reasonable request. But there was no electricity, and therefore no water. Thankfully, a clerk found a candle and guided me down the long dark hall to the washroom.

From the hotel, a runner went to announce our presence on the mountain. Soon Mama Stella Bouette Marealle appeared, walking along the dirt road which connected her home and *shamba* (farm area) with her brother's hotel. We could hear the flip flop of her shoes as she approached us. Mama Stella was dressed in western clothes, but wore a traditional brightly colored cloth head covering—a kanga. Somehow I expected the princess to be more regal even at home, but back in her own surroundings, Mama Stella was just an ordinary Tanzanian woman walking along a dirt path to greet some *wazungu* (plural for mzungu, white) friends. Together we walked to her beautiful home, built by her now deceased husband, an excellent carpenter. The house was filled with beautiful furniture made in her husband's workshop. Seated, she asked us if we wanted a beer or soda. It was so strange—was it a test? Like most Christian missionaries, we did not drink in Tanzania, as whatever we did certainly set the example for all. A cup of beer was 600 =/ (shillings) and the daily wage 1000=/. That would leave 400=/ remaining for the family. It would be next to impossible to feed a family of innumerable children and who knows how many wives with only 400 shillings left.

Her surprised expression took us aback! But we were her guests and never broached the subject with her. That day God put it in my heart to commit to pray for an opportunity to share the life-giving Gospel with her. She had the household things that I needed temporarily, but I had what she needed for eternity.

After our soda, she led us into a huge kitchen area which was loaded with appliances. We were astounded! The room looked like an appliance store: at least four brand new American stoves, several refrigerators, and boxes upon boxes of pots and pans. She showed us a new GE American stove and told us it was ours for the duration of our time in Tanzania. And because most days the electricity doesn't work, she gave us a two-burner gas counter top cooker and a box of high quality pots and pans and utensils, both African and western, to go along. She would even have given us a refrigerator, but when asked if we needed one, we said we had bought one already. She seemed disappointed.

Words can't express our amazement! God was meeting our need through a Chagga woman who, having first evicted us, later took compassion on us. Other missionaries could not believe her generosity. We received blessing upon blessing!

After that we tried to visit her once a year to thank her and to express her part in the Gospel ministry because of the generosity of her loans. One year she told us how much it meant to her, as most of her renters had never come to greet her. Visitation is a huge part of African culture. It might seem such a little thing, but mighty when God's seeds are being sown.

Several years later, when we were planning to return to America because of severe neck and back injuries from the lack of roads, we visited Mama Stella for the last time. Our son, Brian, was going to move across the dirt road to our compound. His compound was much more vulnerable as it backed to the Karanga River. Recently thieves had come up from the river to rob him and his missionary friend, Troy. The thieves' plan was thwarted after a neighboring missionary hearing the commotion fired his rifle into the air several times and dispelled them.

This last safari to Mama Stella's was one of the saddest but joyous of days. It spoke of the finality of our leaving not only Tanzania but passing the missions baton to Brian. As we visited, she again offered us soda, coffee, or tea—never again mentioning the beer. It was with sorrow we told her of our plans to return to the USA. As we told her of Brian's plans to move into our compound, she turned to Brian and asked, "Do you need a stove?" She gladly transferred to Brian all that had been lent to us. And until he left Tanzania years later, that stove was his to use and remained in his home.

As we began to drive away, she stood by the car. I said something about being joined together again one day in heaven. She answered a little sadly that she hoped so, but couldn't be certain. It was the opening I had prayed for all those years, and I jumped into it with Gospel feet. As she stood in her garden, I hung out the window of the car leading her in a confession of faith in Jesus Christ, *that if you confess with your mouth the Lord Jesus and believe in your heart that God has raised Him from the dead, you will be saved. For with the heart one believes unto righteousness, and with the mouth confession is made unto salvation.* (Romans 10: 9-10 NKJV)

God's free gift of salvation was Mama Stella's that glorious day as she confessed her sins, repented before a holy God, and acknowledged her need for the Savior. In the final moments of our friendship, the Holy Spirit made a way. Mama Stella's name was written down in the Lamb's Book of Life as she received Jesus as Savior and Lord. The angels of heaven rejoiced with us!

For by grace are ye saved through faith; and that not of yourselves: it is the gift of God: not of works, lest any man should boast. For we are his workmanship, created in Christ Jesus unto good works, which God hath before ordained that we should walk in them. (Eph. 2:8-10 KJV)

It was a divine connection living on that compound in a furnished house owned by a princess. She had everything but the most important thing, and then suddenly one day as the Holy Spirit opened her understanding, the princess met the King of kings. Wow, what a moment that was! I thank God for the privilege of sharing Jesus with Mama Stella, the woman who gave me her beautiful new white electric stove. It sounds a little crazy, but I loved that electric stove. It was my piece of sanity in a wild and crazy life. Even though it seemed on all the important days the government would turn off our electricity and it wouldn't work, it just didn't matter—it sat there looking like home. Thanks to our benefactor, our *Mountain Mama*, Mama Stella.

Clashes in the Heavenlies

Our visit with Mama Stella had been wonderful. Experiencing her unbelievable generosity, we felt blessed and powerful to proceed like the mighty conquerors God intended us to be— able to take on the world. Well...at least Tanzania. Our first choice of venue was the Tengeru area in the Arusha region. The area was resplendent with lush greenery with a jungle-like appearance. Mount Meru towered in the background, providing life-giving water as well as cool, comfortable night breezes for refreshing sleep. Located in the area was a PEFA church whose pastor told us of an available rental house about two miles away in a tiny village called Patandi. Arrangements were made to visit it. For some unknown reason Swedish Pentecostal missionaries had vacated it suddenly, making it available. The cement block home was partly stucco on the bottom half and the top was freshly painted in the favorite bright African bird's egg shade of blue accented with window frames painted much too brightly with Christmas red. Connected to the front of the house was a large covered veranda with yellow flowering vines draped from post to post along steel wire. Glorious yellow-green and blue feathered sunbirds similar to our hummingbirds loved to visit those vines. The house was charming and inviting; someone had worked hard to make it a home. I loved it at once, except for those red windows. How was it we didn't even notice that a bar was directly across the dirt road?

It was immediately apparent to us that security would be a problem. Although horizontal steel rebar was inserted into the frame of every window, other necessary forms of protection were missing. It was important to have one-inch steel mesh over the outside of every window to deter thieves from using sticks or small children to enter through the four-inch openings between the rebar to remove articles from the room; the rebar only kept larger thieves out. Entering our home was a process. First it was necessary to unlock the ornate steel grillwork security doors which typically had two or three heavy duty tamper-proof locks located at the middle, top, and/or bottom, and then unlock the heavy wooden doors. Inside there were more locks and usually two steel U-shaped brackets inserted in the wall on both sides of the doors into which a board could be placed for additional protection. Those wooden doors alone were more security than any African home would have had, but absolutely insufficient for a *wazungu* home. In third world nations where poverty is rampant, thievery is uncontrollable. Any article—clothing, a tool, whatever—if left outside overnight belonged to someone else by morning. It just went missing! And it was our fault because we left it on display. We had it, and they wanted it—no matter what it was.

Bars, multitudes of locks, and grillwork were necessary fixtures on all openings to prevent break-ins. Some homes even have grillwork doors attached to the inside walls blocking access to the entrance of the bedroom wing. In East Africa, security bars kept the good guys in and the bad guys out; thieves are the ones with the freedom. No matter where we lived, I often thought of prisoners behind bars when I looked outside.

Thieves brandishing razor sharp *pangas* (machetes) were a constant concern. Safety controls were issues we would have to resolve immediately and for which we would be financially responsible. It would be first on our list in addition to building housing for our household staff. If any changes or additions were to be made to the property, the renter paid the tab.

The house had electricity, or at least the necessary wiring if indeed power was available, and of key importance to us, a telephone was prominently displayed in the living room. Unfortunately, it led to a false sense of security. Little did we know, it would rarely operate. Terry and the landlord negotiated the rent and it was settled. We would move in once we paid the rent. Rents in Tanzania vary from prepayment of six months to one year's rent in advance. This can be a shock and true hardship for beginning missionaries. However, all seemed worth it because we were particularly thrilled to know we could live there among the Meru people. What I didn't know was that it had been members of the Meru tribe who had killed the first missionaries in this region years ago, and many remain resistant today to the Gospel light. It was definitely an eerie feeling when I passed by their graves one evening traveling by foot from ministry far up the mountain. Could it possibly have been a warning?

Our first months living there were glorious. I loved walking and praying along the fertile paths surrounded by row upon row of verdant banana trees and long leafy grasses that the village people called *chakula cha ngombe* (cow food). Those tall green grasses were as high as my five-foot-two head. Leaving the forested area and coming down the mountainous terrain, on the other side of that hill a clearing appeared where small groups of Christians were gathered surrounded by the splendor of God's creation. There I would listen in awe of the beauty of their humble praise accompanied only by the simplicity of a drum fashioned from goat skins laced over a hollowed log, played by ordinary sticks plucked from a tree. Such divinely anointed music invited the Holy Spirit's presence all over the land of Tanzania.

Once we had acquired a 4 x 4 Land Rover, we were concerned as to its protection even though it was ten years old. So Terry hired a *fundi* (craftsman of any type) and together they built a garage. One night after the power had gone out they finished the project by placing the heavy steel garage doors in their hinges by candlelight. We always had boxes of white candles for such a power outage. After making puddles of hot wax in a cake pan, I made a flood light by carefully securing the entire box of candles in place and took them out for the men to finish the project. Power in the cities was minimal, but in the village a rarity. We were in for an adventure the likes of which we never again encountered. No power, no water! Terry built a cistern in the back yard where we collected water all through the night even though there was just barely enough pressure for it to trickle into the tank. Villagers got their water from pipes located in various locations throughout the village, usually at the junction of several foot paths. However, someone was always stealing the spigot for resale.

When no bucket was under the faucet, the water ran incessantly wasting away onto the ground. Village everyday life was even more challenging than city life. The electricity was out more often than not shortly after we moved to the village so it was next to impossible to keep food fresh as the fridge was not cold. Circumstances being what they were, I was grateful to soon be going home temporarily to raise increased support for the Moshi Bible School, but felt confident things would be better when we returned. And *eventually* they would be!

With the more powerful 4X4 vehicle, ministry outreach was now possible in distant regions where before it would have been impossible to go because of the roads or rather lack of them. Two of our students at the Bible school, Pastors Nanyaro and James Sirikwa had invited us to visit their area to bring the *Jesus Film* and preach at their churches. Travel to the Manyara-Karatu region located west of Arusha and Moshi toward the Serengeti in the former Subaru was impossible. So when they saw the Land Rover pulling onto the compound during the fall term of the Bible school, their enthusiasm was explosive! They ran to greet us praising God and declaring, "Hallelujah! Now you can come!" Caught up in their enthusiasm we readily accepted the invitation and planned a trip with enormous regional consequences. Unknown to us God was about to plant a seed.

In 1998 the road conditions to the area were at times impassable. Any safari to the top of the Great Rift Valley escarpment where the villages of Karatu and Manyara were located required passing through the river in Mto wa Mbu (River of Mosquitoes), a village at the base of the cliff. Each journey through the river took courage and tenacity! Numerous vehicles stuck up to their bumpers in muck littered the sides of the river. Even trying to find an open, empty space along the shore to attempt the drive across the river was at times next to impossible. It was a long one day journey from the Arusha area just to get to the town; requiring us to spend a night in that village. Darkness was approaching and it was no time to attempt the drive up the escarpment. Terry drove around to many area guest houses trying to find an enclosed compound where not only we, but our vehicle would be safe. What appeared safe in the natural was creepy in the spiritual. Sleep was impossible. Eerie, menacing drums beat all through the night! The atmosphere was negatively charged. Even the faces of the people were hard and twisted; those people were desperately in need of the Light that only Jesus could shine. We were grateful one of our Maasai Bible school students was about to plant a church in Mto wa Mbu.

In the morning, our safari from the base of the escarpment to the village of Manyara at the top continued. We were delighted to be leaving, but the unprotected dangerous switchback road ahead was another adventure waiting for us. All along the steep, rutted, rocky road baboons played and waited for an opportunity for any handout. Huge baobab trees with native orchids in bloom were scattered among the brush along the sides of the road. Part way up the road, there was a pullover where vehicles paused to gaze upon the thousands of pink flamingoes that inhabited the Lake Manyara below. Their pinkish glow reflecting on the lake was breathtaking. In the distance, meandering family groups of elephants and giraffes could also be seen. We were in awe of God and His creation!

We loved the spacious freedom and pristine wildness of the region, but the switchback road was one of the most hazardous places to travel in East Africa. The grade was a severe challenge for overloaded trucks and buses which repeatedly lost their brakes while trying to navigate the steepness and the switchback curves. Once we were stunned to see a bus literally dangling over the edge suspended on a tree trunk. In situations like that, for self-preservation the Tanzanians would courageously jump out the windows as their bus speedily rolled backward.

At the top of the escarpment overlooking Lake Manyara National Park stood the little village of Manyara. In the evening we were to show the *Jesus Film* on the Manyara Village clearing. By day it was a playful soccer field, but by night the field became holy ground. Many Iraqw villagers responded to the Gospel that night. Seven years later, ten of those who had met Jesus as Savior that November evening in 1998 would be students of the future Lake Manyara Christian College and Pastor Nanyaro would one day be its principal.

After returning home from the villages with the October Bible school session complete and our ministry promise fulfilled, Terry locked our vehicle in the newly built garage, handed the property keys over to Longida, our trusted Maasai household worker, and we went home to raise increased support for the management of the Moshi PEFA Bible School. Following the New Year we returned, eager to begin what would now become our own missionary work. We were no longer just relief missionaries; we were the real thing. As we landed, I remember asking the airline hostess if she had any matches as

I noticed the lights were out again. I could not imagine trying to find our way in the house without light. Missionary friends picked us up at the airport and took us home. That day they had given Longida the keys so he could open the house and begin the process of cleaning the dusty cement floors. Although we certainly trusted him completely, it would have been unsafe for him to personally have held the keys the entire time we were gone. We loved Longida; he had become a faithful son to us.

We honked at the gate to announce our presence. Smiling brightly, Longida came running to unlock the compound steel gates, the steel security grill doors on the front door, and finally the wooden doors behind it. Everyone on the compound was there to greet us, but we sensed some attitudes were different. When we had moved from the compound in Arusha, we moved with us the staff of three we had inherited from the Cliffs, a family of five. Peter and Longida worked outside doing gardening and laundry while Rose worked in the kitchen. Our new compound was very small and three workers were certainly not needed, but the people moving onto our former compound didn't need them. Out of mercy for their welfare, we moved them with us; however, the cousins were very offended that we had moved them to the village, calling it a *shamba* (farm). Rose and Peter were city folk and they didn't like being isolated in Patandi Village. They resented the present conditions more than we could have imagined. Before we left for furlough we had begun to notice a slight change in Peter, so we had given the coveted keys—a sign of authority and rank to the younger Longida.

Terry remained outside to check on things in the compound. Exhausted after the 20-something hours on three different flights, I went immediately to the bedroom to get ready to retire for the night. For some reason I opened my closet door on my way past it as I proceeded into the master bathroom to remove my contact lenses from dry weary eyes. Being tired I forgot to take my glasses with me into the bathroom. When I returned to the bedroom, I noticed a *belt* had fallen from the closet. As I bent over to pick it up, I clearly heard a voice in my spirit say, "Don't touch that." Simultaneously, as I reversed my action the *belt* came alive and proceeded to raise its foul snake head in my direction. Quickly retracting my hand, I let out a bloodcurdling scream as I waited for rescue. Terry came running, went to the side of the bed where he always kept a *panga* for added personal protection, and proceeded to whack the snake until it appeared lifeless, and then left. It began moving again, so taking the words of Jesus to heart and quoting scripture from Luke 10:19, "*Behold, I give unto you power to tread on serpents and scorpions, and over all the power of the enemy: and nothing shall by any means hurt you,*" (KJV) I repeatedly stomped on the snake's head until it moved no more. What a welcome home surprise! That year we brought Rachel Fortner home with us, and I am sure that was more than she bargained for. But, brave soul that she was, each night she would climb under her mosquito netting, tuck it in around her mattress, and confess nothing could get to her there.

A couple days later as I was washing my feet in the master bathroom tub (a frequent event in a dusty culture), another surprise awaited me. When the *fundi ya magi* (plumber) installed the tub, he put the faucets on the wrong side of the tub to the right and the drain on the opposite side to the left. Facing the faucet, I was busily washing my feet when in my peripheral vision I saw something black and familiar looking coming out of the drain and into the tub. By the time I saw it at least 6-8 inches of snake was precisely where I wanted to be. Bloodcurdling scream number two was followed by Terry yelling, "Now what?"

Later that day, when it was time for Rachel to shower in the guest bathroom, I had a tugging feeling we should check it. The bathroom consisted of a porcelain toilet in the left corner with an open floor drain in the corner on the other side. The shower was merely a pipe sticking out of the wall with a shower head attached. The water ran onto the cement floor. There was a slight groove formed in the cement to direct the water toward the drain in the corner. At the opening of the door was a two inch ledge which kept the water from running down the hallway and into our living room. Inside the bathroom we used to keep a multi-purpose bright red round plastic tub in the corner over the drain. It was great for hand-washing of clothes and collecting extra water for shaving or foot washing. As the evening wore on, I kept asking Terry to go in and check it. Repeatedly he kept saying I was being overly cautious, that surely another snake would not be in the house.

The nagging feeling just wouldn't leave me, so I got the broom to use the handle to flip over the red basin. Rachel and I, standing as far away as possible and looking ridiculously helpless, moved Terry to come and relieve our anxieties. He was about to lift the tub with his bare hands when I begged him to use the broom, and there waiting for us was snake number three. Another scream, but this time Rachel joined the chorus. Finally, the last one appeared in the toilet a few days later as I turned around to flush. For a long time thereafter, I first looked into a toilet before using it. A few weeks later when Rachel's parents, Jeff and Maureen Fortner, came to visit, the problem was solved. Jeff is great American *fundi*. He and Terry used plastic margarine containers to make traps outside which allowed water to escape but kept unwanted varmints from entering through the drainage pipes. Every missionary has a snake story and I hoped that would be the end of mine. No way!

In the weeks that followed we had many strange occurrences beginning with having to release Rose and Peter from service. I was heartbroken. Together we had done *Jesus Film* ministry, and they were such a huge part of our lives that first year. We had forgiven their former rebellious behaviors, but their negative attitudes and uncooperativeness toward our houseguests could not be tolerated. Tanzania is all about hospitality.

The second attack came in a physical way. My first month in Tanzania I had made a request of God. "Now Lord if you want me out there in the bush using holes in the ground for a potty, would You please turn my premenopausal state to a post-menopausal one—complete pause, meaning over and done!" Graciously, my request had been answered and it was one for which I was very grateful.

At first I hated using a *choo*, which was basically a thirty foot hole in the ground. *Vyoo* (plural for *choo*) came in different varieties: some were a hole in the center of a cement floor with two places designated for feet; others were temporary, a shallow hole surrounded by cloth for privacy; and the worst were the very rickety, rotted wooden platforms suspended over many years worth of putrefied yuck. Trying to figure out which direction to face and where to place my feet was a challenge. Then there was the issue of holding up the dress while at the same time clutching the undies to the side and holding onto the toilet paper (if I had not forgotten to bring it). All this while I was trying to aim properly in order to keep my feet dry. Not to ignore the buzzing flies who had just visited the pile below or the random, hidden vampire mosquito trying to bite my now exposed derriere. It was not a pretty picture!

While we were living in Patandi village, suddenly for no reason my bleeding returned and continued for almost a month. The hemorrhage was draining my strength. I knew it was not natural, for as the Bible puts it I had ceased to be *after the manner of women.* (Gen. 18:11 KJV) It just wouldn't stop. (And remember there is no corner drug store.) Traveling became difficult for me so I decided to remain at home one evening when Terry went to minister the *Jesus Film* in an Anglican bush church. In my weakened state, I just rested on the bed praying for Terry, the lost souls coming to the film, and me! I knew the Lord had answered my prayer to stop this bleeding thing —so how could this be happening again? It was at that precise moment that the Lord reminded me of a testimony I had read in Watchman Nee's book, *The Latent Power of the Soul.* What a miracle! The book was on our shelf just waiting for this critical moment in time. God knew I would need it, and He had me pack it! Immediately, I found the strength to rise out of bed and go to our bookshelf to get it. Finding the little book, I crawled back into bed. Diligently I searched for the part concerning the soul power force coming against a woman. Quickly I read the book until I rediscovered the pertinent paragraph on page 48 where Nee talks of a woman with a similar problem to mine. The Lord had revealed to that woman that a group of deceived women, who were in opposition to her, had been "praying" about her. They had been praying according to their own will and not God's will for her. Their soulish prayer had released the devil to manifest his destructive devices toward her, an innocent victim. God directed her to break the power of their psychic prayer coming against her and cut it off by faith in the power of the blood of Christ.

I prayed the prayer she had prayed and immediately my bleeding ceased and never returned. I had learned a huge lesson about the power of soulish prayer and its negative physical effect on others. A person not lead by the Holy Spirit in prayer, who persists in praying his or her own personal will concerning a situation, can release the devil to manifest his destructive devices. Someone's soul power was being unleashed against me.

Jesus taught us to pray in line with the Father's will. God always answers our prayers righteously and never makes a mistake. "Praying" our will and *not* God's will into a situation is a form of witchcraft whether it is done in Africa or America.

When we pray our will, we circumvent the omniscience of God, step onto His throne, and take another's life into our hands— even releasing demonic forces against him or her. When Jesus taught his disciples to pray, He said, *"Your kingdom come. Your will be done on earth as it is in heaven."* (Matt. 6:10 NKJV)

While the bleeding issue was continuing for a month inside the house, outside our thorn-bush hedge was being repeatedly slashed through with holes. The hedge is the first line of defense against intruders of all shapes and sizes, and the holes were big enough for the neighbors' chickens to wander in and our dogs to wander out. And, of course, overly protective guard dogs and chickens don't mix; our German shepherds would savagely mangle the invading chicken. The neighbors would then demand we recompense them for their uninvited damaged chicken and then promptly take it home, cook, and eat it. After a repeat of this chaotic episode, I finally went out and had a serious talk with Longida, asking him again to please firmly tell the gardener **not** to cut the hedge! He quietly listened, saying nothing. Africans are very loyal to one another, but in this case I think he was fearful of reporting the truth of the incident—that it was the landlord who had been the one repeatedly cutting holes in our hedge. Longida was a righteous man, and eventually he did tell us. It seemed weird, but there was no time to deal with that information. More visitors were on their way, and we were busy making preparations.

In June 1998 we were blessed with two mission teams from central New York. Team 1 was a construction team led by Pastor Chris Lonneville and Paul Schultz, who came to build a multi-purpose room at the PEFA Moshi Bible School and two women who taught on worship. After Team 1, including Terry and the Land Rover, moved to Moshi, another team consisting of three young women led by Pastor Lee and Averell Simmons arrived. It was a crazily busy time, but looking back we clearly see God's gracious provision. Unknown to us God was using both teams to bring about His perfect plan for us.

While Team 1 was working hard in Moshi, Team 2 and I did seminars with the local PEFA church in Nguruma about a thirty minute walk from our Patandi village home. The year before we had shown the *Jesus Film* in the Nguruma and forty-eight people had given their lives to Jesus. Now we were returning to teach and encourage the members of the growing church. Days later after returning home one afternoon, I discovered our normally irregular phone service down again, at first I wasn't alarmed. The incident with the hedge was forgotten in the past. Suddenly, our dogs became extremely ill, and soon we saw them begin to hemorrhage. Averell, a nurse, was the first to mention the dogs' eyes had become jaundiced. Someone had poisoned them. We anointed and prayed over them and believed for a miracle. Both dogs responded favorably for a time. Although I had heard that it was not uncommon for thieves to kill missionaries' dogs so they could rob them, when local lore becomes your own personal reality, it is indeed scary, emotionally distressing, and painful.

For several days while walking back and forth along the mountainous paths to the Nguruma village church, we had joyfully prayed, laughed, and sang God's praise. Everyone in the local area had seen or heard us! Someone sinister was not only aware of their presence in my home, but also knew the *mzungu* woman was on her own as the *bwana* (mister) was more than an hour away in Moshi. Now I was starting to be very concerned, as here we six were under an enormous attack with Terry oblivious in Moshi. We were isolated and alone and out of touch with civilization. I was alone and in charge with five visitors in my home, and three of them were beautiful young women. That alone frightened me! Midweek came and the team left for their previously scheduled safari to view the magnificent wildlife of Tanzania. At the time it never occurred to me that I should have just jumped in the car and worried about the financial cost later. But the Lord had something else in store for me—a lesson of His great love and faithfulness in the midst of an impossible situation. Behind the scenes God was at work!

I was home alone. Thankful the missions team, particularly those young women, were safe. I still felt a bit—no, more than a bit—terrified of the unknown concerning my own personal future. I knew God was faithful and tonight the test was on—how strong was my belief in the provision of a God who cannot lie? It was definitely a Psalm 91 kind of day.

He who dwells in the shelter of the Most High will rest in the shadow of the Almighty. I will say of the Lord, "He is my refuge and my fortress, my God, in whom I trust." "... You will not fear the terror of night," (Psalm 91: 1-2, 5)

As soon as they departed, I began to radically cry out to God, *"Please speak to Terry and please, God, bring him home...NOW!"* I don't remember exactly what I did, but that was probably one of those times when my home alone ritual would go into effect. I would climb under my mosquito net with a flashlight handy. Taking my Bible, I would read it and then lay it open over my heart. Then I would pray for the Lord to send His holy angels to protect me. Then with the authority that Jesus gave to His disciples, I would bind every assignment of Satan against me. Finally surrendering to the Holy Spirit's nudging, I would once more declare God's sovereignty in all things and rest in Him!

There was a grace in those hours that only a loving God could give. There was no music, certainly no television, no cell phone, and iPods hadn't been invented, so being alone was terribly alone, except for the hope that only Jesus can give. In spite of how things appeared in the natural, I had the assurance that God remains faithful to perform His Word. I had a promise that He would never leave me nor forsake me. No matter how hopeless my circumstances appeared, God was still on the throne.

Very early the next morning, Terry arrived. There was an urgency about him. Now I realize he wondered how I would react to his forthcoming news. I fell into his arms emotionally exhausted from the terror while weeping with gratitude to God for a divine deliverance. Quickly the details of the past few days emerged as I began to relate to him our potentially serious situation. Miraculously, God had revealed to him the necessity of our moving to Moshi, and he had already made arrangements for us to view a rental home there. Basically he came home to tell me we were moving, and I was waiting to tell him—get us out of here NOW! God had revealed His plan for our safety. Now we needed to walk out the details. Terry and Longida loaded our now limp, hemorrhaging guard dogs into the back of the Land Rover to go into Arusha town with the hopes of locating a veterinarian. One dog died on the way and the other died shortly thereafter as no help was available. It was the lowest point of the week, but more trouble was yet to come as the enemy's plans unfolded.

Sometime during the early afternoon the electricity had been cut at the pole along with the phone line. Now there was no possibility of power or communication. And soon our guests would return hungry. I was grateful for the gas two-burner counter-top cooker compliments of Mama Stella. My heart was so saddened by the death of the dogs; it was almost impossible to be able to just plan dinner let alone cook it. We were thoroughly stressed! We knew soon Team 2 would arrive home from their wildlife safari; we had much to tell them. And most of it wasn't good!

No phone, no electricity, and dusk was approaching. It was 6:30 in the evening and we faced almost twelve hours of impenetrable blackness until daybreak the next morning. No street lights, no car lights—nothing but a few lanterns here and there. Evacuation was impossible that day. When the team returned, they were bubbling with excitement over their wildlife safari. At once they realized the dogs were dead. Dread filled the air. Everyone knew the consequences of the dogs' demise were dire. We ate quickly and entered into a time of prayer.

We were vacillating between peace with trust and fear. The darker it became outside the more our anxiety increased. Suddenly, there was a greeting at the gate. Father God had sent a company of men. Each man carried a lantern from the Nguruma village where we had sown God's redemptive seed. Redemption follows redemption.

The village ministry had been a great time! Young American women crossing cultural barriers with one ingredient—love. The village children were thrilled by their first experiences with brightly colored crafts; some were so excited they even nibbled on the crayons. But it was the love they felt from hugs so generously given that was touching them most. Meanwhile Lee, Averell, and I were teaching seminars inside the precious church. Nguruma's village church building was more like a shelter with plank walls half-way topped by plastic blue pieces tied from post to post to keep the rain or dust out, depending upon the season. Inside there were very short wooden benches, a mud floor, and colorful bougainvillea boughs strung all around celebrating the American visitors. Visitors always attracted a crowd and the Simmons' visit that first Sunday was no exception. As the worship music started and the congregation began to move and celebrate in true African style, a woman began to roll on the floor and foam at the mouth. Demons cannot abide the presence of the Holy Spirit; when the anointing flows, demons manifest. Fortunately, the pastor had been part of my doctrine of angels class when we discussed the handling of such a situation—a designated person to quietly remove the manifesting person from the church. It happened to be a woman, so Averell and I ministered to her and in the mighty name of Jesus she was marvelously set free. Blessing upon blessing and for the first time God gave Averell the gift of tongues—right when she needed it most. It was a great time of celebrating the wonder of a Holy God!

We were all so blessed to be a part of encouraging those precious saints. Even as we had encouraged them through the seminars for the men, women, and children, they now came to the compound to encourage us. All night they prayed, sang, and walked the property. They stationed themselves as sentries at the gate, around the perimeter, and in front of the doors. Inside all of us were praying with them, but additionally we thanked God for His divine provision of those wonderful caring warriors. How they knew to come to our rescue only heaven knows.

The next morning Terry went to a missionary friend's house to telephone Steve and Anne Street and make arrangements to secure the young women there. Together we all drove the girls to Moshi. While there, Terry showed me the rental house he had seen; we finalized the rental agreement and arranged to move in later that week. There was still more ministry to be done in Nguruma. On the way home from Moshi Terry related to the Simmons and me the events of his week with the men and women from Team 1. While constructing the multi-purpose building, the team became an answer to prayer in many ways, as God used them to help us solve more than one problem. Our biggest ministry problem was with the pastor of the Bible school campus church. His deceased father had been the former national overseer of PEFA. In Tanzanian culture, sons of important leaders are traditionally granted favor and position regardless of whether they deserve it or not. Thus he had favor with the new national leadership. For over a year we observed some things that made us question his integrity. Red flags were popping up all over! The spirit within him clashed with our spirits whenever he translated for us as we preached. During one visit by the PEFA overseer, he was chosen by the overseer to be the weeklong translator for the preaching and pastor wives' conferences, even though we had requested

Pastor Lazaro. We had noticed he was just too familiar toward women; without proof we were powerless to replace him.

One day while waiting for the cement lintels over the doors and windows to dry, the Moshi building team went for a walk into the nearby forest to view the dynamic black and white colobus monkeys. Pastor Chris decided to remain back at the compound in the men's dormitory building; he was out of sight. When he came out of the building, he noticed the campus pastor touching the cook inappropriately as she was trying to prepare meals for the guest team. Deeply grieved, Chris held the information trying to decide when and how to tell us. Later in the week, when Paul and the campus pastor went shopping for some supplies, he observed some shenanigans with money. Humbly they came to us expecting us to be devastated only to find out we had been praying for God to either bring him to repentance or remove him from the compound. We would need to deal with him after the teams left.

In the afternoon the four of us returned to Patandi to complete the village ministry we had planned in Nguruma, and pray for a plan to end the problem at the church. The next day a women's conference was scheduled at the church; Averell had some teachings designed especially for young mothers. Even if we had wanted to, there was no way to cancel it; there was literally no way to communicate with the women. But most importantly we had to obey the word of the Lord that says in Psalm15:4, "...*He who swears to his own hurt and does not change*" NKJV. It would have been devastating to them if we had not come. They had walked for miles to attend, expecting something from the Lord through His servants, whom everyone now knew had God's power to cast out devils.

Again at dusk the faithful praying men returned. All of us rested better knowing they were there, the girls were safe in Moshi, and that God had provided our way of escape—a new home in Moshi. Immediately after sun rise the next morning, our missionary friend, Mike Rothery, began honking frantically at our gate. He came from Arusha town warning us to get out now; they were coming to get us! One of Mike's friends, a pastor from the Mount Meru region, had been advised of the secret plans to attack us and had hastened to Mike with the urgent message. Longida went to get my dearest Tanzanian friend, Eli Kiriama. She worked together with our new household worker, Neema, to pack my belongings and all the loose household stuff. Meanwhile Averell and I walked to the church to do the women's conference. From the moment the anointing hit, I never even thought about what was happening at home—the fact that the devil was trying to destroy us, our ministry, and everything we had, as minimal as it was. God's grace covered my heart and mind completely. But as soon as the final amen was pronounced, trepidation again entered my soul. Quickly, the two of us crossed the mountainous footpaths unsure of what we would find. Arriving at the gate, stomach in my throat, I saw Mike's 4 x 4 covered in furniture and our Land Rover also loaded to the hilt. Things were sticking out all over tied to the top, the back, and the sides. Half-way to Moshi, our, or rather Mama Stella's, coffee table crashed to the ground. That was the only material casualty.

Bible school would begin in a week. There was no time to process the pain. There is just no time for self-pity when there is no time for self. It was just one more painful layer covered over by endless days of demanding activity. The lingering loss of watching our dogs' decline, the hopeful sign of recovery, and then their imminent deaths was an excruciatingly painful experience. They were poisoned for a second time days later while we were at church. In the end they were too weak to withstand its power.

Shortly after our move to Moshi, dear British friends, who came to say *pole* (sorry for the troubles), told us about their neighbors' German shepherd who just had had a litter of puppies. We made arrangements to see them the next weekend. There was a long-haired fat, fluffy puppy who tugged at our heart. That day we adopted the greatest pet we have ever owned. We named her Baraka, which means blessing. Being now a little overly protective, little Baraka lived on the front screened-in veranda. One day as I let her out and turned to go back into the house, I felt a check in my spirit for her safety. As I exited the veranda door, I interrupted an eagle's flight path intending a direct hit on our sweet puppy. God is faithful even to rescue His creation. Along with the prayers of the saints, her puppy antics drove the pain away and joy began to return to our souls. Early on, Terry slept on the couch on our screened veranda with her so all of us, including the neighbors, could get some rest. One morning he awoke to find her mouth full of screen. That day she went outside to fulfill her duty in the world of big guard dogs.

Many are the afflictions of the righteous, but the LORD delivers him out of them all. (Psalm 34:19 NKJV)

The righteous cry out, and the LORD hears, and delivers them out of all their troubles. (Psalm 34:17 NKJV)

Women's Ministry: A Call for Resurrection

One day during our first months of living in Arusha, God called me to a fast. After earnestly fasting and praying, I had gone outside to walk and pray in the garden. Walking along the edge of our bougainvillea thorn hedge, I felt the presence of God as a fire rising within me. Suddenly, I began to pray in a tongue I had never experienced before; it was powerful and warlike. With arms swinging, I was marching back and forth fighting in a language that I did not understand. Violent words had flowed from my spirit. Jesus explained it like this: *"The kingdom of heaven suffers violence, and the violent take it by force."* (Matt. 11:12 NKJV) After the urgency passed, I asked the Lord for whom I was praying and He told me, "You are praying for the women of Africa."

God had a mighty plan for the women of Tanzania, and that day He had privileged me with the burden of praying for them. Something new had been birthed in me. Those mamas (women) were now in my heart; it was a deep planting. Jesus had planted a seed in my spirit, but it would be up to Him to bring forth the harvest. It took years to plow up the fallow ground in ways unimaginable to me. Now I understand that there were two main hindrances impeding the fulfillment of that prayer; both obstacles were being broken and reshaped in the Master's hands for the appointed time. The first was the African men's cultural attitudes toward women. God's idea of matrimony is that marriage is a covenant, a tri-fold promise made among a husband, a wife, and Himself. A covenant is not to be broken. Marriage in Tanzania was a contract. Contracts can be broken. A woman was a product—bought, sold, and returned if defective. There is no concept in the Swahili language for romantic love. Many women were merely purchased for sex and procreation, and what would be considered slave labor in any western culture. Females were mere property belonging first to the family to use as they wished and then later sold to a man for whom she would procreate. It was not love; it was an arranged contract. If the poor soul bore no children, even if *he* were the infertile one, she would then be banished and another wife taken. Where could she go? Her family did not want her as she would be merely another mouth to feed. For many prostitution was then their fate until AIDS would take its toll. Such was the value of women.

Reminiscing over the years, I now understand why it was so difficult for some of the men to be taught by me, a woman. Being accepted into ministry in Tanzania was a struggle. In America I was the Bible teacher and Terry was a professor. Arriving in Tanzania, the ministry and teaching roles became his. In America I was the one with the ministry credentials and the Bible education, but in Tanzania I was the *wrong gender*.

To accept me as a valuable individual—worse yet a preacher— would have turned their world upside down. I was asking for acceptance in a place where it had not been given before. I was expecting the impossible. That is exactly what women of faith do—believe God to do the impossible and make a way in the wilderness of life. Women were bought and sold—a mere a piece of property! If a woman had no value, how could she possibly have anything to teach a man?

Such was the societal atmosphere upon which I *intruded* the first time I walked into the Moshi PEFA Bible School in June of 1997. It was oppressive. Many sat with arms folded, totally closed to anything I had to say. They basically dared me to teach them anything. Who was this *mzungu* anyway? And who does she think she is to stand in front of men—let alone pastors? It was dreadful. I was so depressed as I had conscientiously prepared and was maybe even expecting to be appreciated—perhaps even applauded—for my sacrifice. After all, I was a missionary with a Master's degree, I had been to Bible school and furthermore, hadn't I left my family, sold my home and all my wonderful stuff? I just wasn't ready for all that rejection. Pride is so deceptive.

For I say, through the grace given to me...not to think of himself more highly than he ought to think, but to think soberly. (Rom. 12:3 NKJV)

God was producing one more attitudinal change in me. All is for Him and by Him for His glory! I was just a vessel; He could work through me only if I remained broken and surrendered. There was a popular song then—*It's not about me that He should do things my way.* That was the new theme of my life. And I was indeed frustrated!

Yes, the men had a problem—a big one, but I was the other obstacle in the equation—a woman shaped by western values and ideas. Marilyn Weaver needed to die to self so that the broken servant God intended to use—would come forth. Finally at the breaking point, I had come to the end of myself, surrender was imminent. So on the Sunday morning before school began, as I sat staring at the raised platform inside campus church, I told the Lord, "God, I don't care if I ever preach again." He responded, "Now, you will preach!"

Attitudes inside the classroom remained the same. Monday and Tuesday they continued to sit with arms folded and minds closed. By Wednesday morning I was despondent. Driving down to the campus with a heart of spiritual despair I said to the Lord, "If you don't do something today, I will die." I had to be completely surrendered to Him—His ideas and His ways. Death would bring life. Jesus explained it this way: *"I tell you the truth, unless a kernel of wheat falls to the ground and dies, it remains only a single seed. But if it dies, it produces many seeds."* (John 12:24 NIV)

Desperation with humiliation moved the hand of God! As I stepped on the threshold of the building, courage to go in mounted up within my being as I knew somehow God would confirm my anointing before them that day. Suddenly, as I was teaching, the Holy Spirit fell in a phenomenal way. As the tangible presence of the Holy Spirit filled the classroom, precious men of God cried in repentance at their resistance to the will of God. There were puddles of their tears on the cement floor. Even now I can see them kneeling, weeping as the Spirit of God washed over their souls. God's favor changes everything. No situation is beyond our transcendent God. When God confirms a ministry, it is an indisputable thing.

Fear not, for I am with you; Be not dismayed, for I am your God. I will strengthen you, Yes, I will help you, I will uphold you with My righteous right hand. Behold, all those who were incensed against you, shall be ashamed... (Isa. 41:10 NKJV)

In God's timing, on the third day of my first class at the Moshi PEFA Bible School, He poured out His favor. That day the Holy Spirit made it abundantly clear that He had anointed me and called me to that place. God opened the door in His timing. It was the beginning of a breakthrough for any woman of Tanzania who was held spiritually captive. God had paved the way; men formerly in bondage to the devil's lies concerning gender would now begin to acknowledge that women had worth.

"Not by might nor by power, but by My Spirit," says the LORD *of hosts.* (Zech. 4:6 KJV)   Truly God was the only One who could make the way. He loves to do the impossible! *"And it shall come to pass in the last days," says God, "That I will pour out of My Spirit on all flesh; your sons and* **your daughters** *shall prophesy, your young men shall see visions, your old men shall dream dreams. And on My menservants and on* **My maidservants** *I will pour out My Spirit in those days; and they shall prophesy."* (Acts 2:17-18)

It took years of plowing. Daily dying to self, meant doing culturally acceptable things such as wearing skirts or dresses everywhere, head coverings in the mountain villages, and being an unopinionated, submissive woman. That was very hard for me, and most times I didn't succeed very well. It wasn't until I finally realized only prayer could change the things that really needed changing that I began to fully cooperate with God. It took years to give up rights to an

117

opinion. Finally I learned it was more profitable to discuss behind closed doors at home with my husband those things which culturally needed to be altered and then let the changes be implemented through him. One of the first areas needing change was the husband and wife issue Sunday mornings at the local church. The first Sunday at church Terry marched out with all the men and I was left on the platform. Many couples wouldn't even sit together. On the way home that first day I said to Terry, "From now on let's walk out together." From then on if I was on sitting on the platform, he would wait for me and if I was sitting in the audience, he would stop at my seat and invite me to walk with him. By demonstrating honor we began to teach them to value their wives.

There were many other things that greatly stressed me about the culture—like female circumcision. Just the thought was so painful that I had to put it out of my mind and obey God. God had an order. First to come would be the knowledge of a Savior. We were there to preach and teach the Gospel message of salvation. The rest was God's job in God's time. We were to obey Him and leave cultural changes to the powerful transforming ministry of the Holy Spirit.

From that day forward my prayers were to water the seed God planted in my heart, even if I did not yet fully comprehend what would come from it. After moving to Moshi, God opened the door for me to begin to do more village women's conferences—my favorite of all ministries. These were God's beautiful Tanzanian women entrusted to me. It was a privilege. Yet the caution from the Apostle James was often on my mind,

"... you know that we who teach will be judged more strictly." (James 3:1 NIV)

My first conference was among the Meru women in Legaruki. We had shown the *Jesus Film* there on July fourth the previous year. It was a startling experience. The first day was proceeding wonderfully. We were experiencing the power of God when suddenly a regional overseer came in, walked to the platform, and demanded lunch. Our conferences were always accompanied by healthy lunches. Those precious saints had walked for many miles to attend with nothing but perhaps tea for sustenance. Knowing the ladies came on empty stomachs, we gladly fed them physically as well as spiritually. That pastor's total disregard for the Holy Spirit's presence quenched the anointing and the meeting ended abruptly.

The second day was a Holy Ghost explosion. Unlike the overseer, these ladies had tasted God the day before. They came hungry for more of Him. A massive move of intercession such as I had never seen before broke out. As they began weeping before the King of kings, the Holy Spirit directed me to have the women face their homes as they prayed. The huge crowd faced every direction interceding in unison for their loved ones. Set free from the tragedies of everyday life, the women began to worship in Spirit and truth. Transformed by the power of God, everywhere ladies began falling under the power of God as the wind of the Holy Spirit swept across the room. Later, after Holy Communion, the Holy Spirit fell again. Many began to shake and fall as the power of the Holy Spirit hovered over them. One woman just began to dance before the Lord. It was beautiful. The anointing was powerful; the movement continued for several hours. Inexpressible joy filled the room. Area pastors, who had heard from their women that God was in the house came hungry—not to partake of lunch but God. Humbly they entered, sat in the rear of the church building, and drank from the river of life. They were ablaze with the Spirit's glow. That day no one, not even the men, cared about lunch! We had all eaten of the Bread of Life and were full.

Women's conferences were now not only acceptable but following the Holy Ghost explosion at Legaruki requested. Opportunities opened up in many churches. Sometime later a PEFA women's leader came to a meeting. In English she said the following words to me, "I heard about you. I came to see you. You are the only anointed white woman I have ever heard." Again God was confirming that He was in this thing! It wasn't me—it was Jesus. And now was His time for them!

In a tiny village high up in the Arumeru District, the highlands between Mt Kilimanjaro and Mt Meru there was a whitewashed mud and stick PEFA church perched noticeably along the side of the road. One day as I was there doing a one day women's conference teaching on Queen Esther, I began to share with the women how fasting and prayer had brought her favor with the king and how the king had lowered his scepter toward Esther ushering her into his presence in order to grant her request. Using Esther's situation to build their faith, I felt led by the Holy Spirit to encourage them as daughters of the King of kings to remember that when Jesus died on the cross and the temple curtain was rent that He opened the way for ladies to come into His presence with their requests. And they were to believe King Jesus would answer them. Faith to believe God at His word had been released among them.

Soon after that a woman came into the meeting carrying her small infirm child. Immediately I recognized the problem. He definitely had *slim's disease*, a Swahili euphemism for AIDS. His young body was literally bones wrapped in skin. He laid there limp resting in his mother's arms his clothing draped loosely around him. His bulging eyes watered, mucous ran from his nose, and droll poured from his mouth. Kathy Bragg who had accompanied me that day had brought lollipops for all the children and she gave him one. More droll! Liquids carrying the dreaded AIDS virus oozed from every possible body orifice.

Immediately I knew what she wanted, *but I didn't yet know who she was*. One of the many wonderful things about the village people is their pure unadulterated faith. God said it and they totally believed it—and the missionary, God's emissary was sent there to perform it.

Jesus' final words to His disciples exhorted them to *"go into all the world and preach the gospel to every creature. He who believes and is baptized will be saved; but he who does not believe will be condemned. And these signs will follow those who believe: In My name they will cast out demons; they will speak with new tongues; they will take up serpents; and if they drink anything deadly, it will by no means hurt them; they will lay hands on the sick, and they will recover."* (Mark 16:15-18 NKJV)

Many would think such powerful words would inspire tremendous faith. Unfortunately sometimes quite the contrary can be true. Fear of man and fear of failure often dominate the psyche before pride dissolves and faith arises. Oh the preaching part is easy, especially overseas where everyone hangs on your very words; it's the last part—the part that says *they will recover* that can make a preacher quake. What if they don't?

Terror gripped my heart! Fleshly fear was trying to override any compassion for the precious dying child. Faith was ebbing away. Suddenly the Holy Spirit reminded me of a promise He had planted in my heart over ten years before.

One morning during my normal devotional reading, I had read Psalm 91. There was an inner voice that said to me, "Now read it again!" In verses 5-8 *You shall not be afraid of the terror by night, nor of the arrow that flies by day, nor of the pestilence that walks in darkness, nor of the destruction that lays waste at noonday. A thousand may fall at your side, and ten thousand at your right hand; But it shall not come near you. Only with your eyes shall you look, and see the reward of the wicked.* (NKJV) As I did, I clearly heard the Lord speak to my innermost being, "This is my promise to you and your family about the AIDS virus." The memory of that promise quickened me! God was so gracious. My moment of wavering faithlessness did not in the least cancel God's faithful mercy for this precious woman and her dying son or even me. In God's sovereign message of love to me years ago was the nugget of peace I needed. Faith in the healing redeeming power of God began to arise in me! Fearlessly I was then able to lay my hands on the AIDS laden child. In the name of Jesus I cursed the disease at the root and prayed for him to live. Years later I found out the power of God touched that child and he was completely healed.

What I didn't know was that his mother was the woman I had prayed for a year before and God had miraculously healed her of the same disease. The woman facing me that afternoon was the personification of health—robust in stature, hopeful in spirit. Faith drew her to the conference because she knew the healing power of Jesus! She was herself—a radiant living miracle.

Her faith was strong; mine, on the other hand, was like the father who cried out to Jesus, *"Lord, help thou my unbelief!"* God's help was there for me before I ever breathed a prayer. The mother's miracle had been the result of a word of knowledge the year before. We had taken Pastor John Wentworth there to preach on a Sunday morning. Following the preaching, God had given me a word for the church that there was a woman dying of AIDS present in the service, but that she was not guilty. Her husband had brought it home to her and that if she came forward that day, God would heal her. Mobs of people came forward for prayer; we had no idea which one was the person God was pinpointing. The Village did! She did! And certainly God Almighty did!

Two days later the local pastor came down to report that miracle! Talking to us on our veranda, he exclaimed, *"Baba na mama, everyone in the village is talking about the mzungu woman who must be a prophet! The dying woman is alive and well. She is eating and doing all her own chores again—the whole village is talking about it! We are all praising the Lord!"*

That woman was the young mother who carried the frail male child overcome by *slim's disease.* Her son had contracted the

AIDS virus in her womb. In her heart she knew Father God was no respecter of persons, and that because of the sacrificial death of His Son, her son could live! Surely, Jesus desired to touch her son even as He had miraculously touched her the year before. And He did!

Years later at a pastors' wives conference at the Kilimanjaro Christian College, I asked the Arumeru village pastor's wife, "How is the boy and his mother?" *"Wazima! Wote ni wazima kabisa!"* ("All are completely healthy and well!") was the reply. Truly mustard seed faith can move mountains.

Psalm 91

He who dwells in the secret place of the Most High shall abide under the shadow of the Almighty. I will say of the LORD, "He is my refuge and my fortress; My God, in Him I will trust." Surely He shall deliver you from the snare of the fowler, and from the perilous pestilence. He shall cover you with His feathers. And under His wings you shall take refuge; His truth shall be your shield and buckler. You shall not be afraid of the terror by night, nor of the arrow that flies by day, nor of the pestilence that walks in darkness, nor of the destruction that lays waste at noonday.

A thousand may fall at your side, and ten thousand at your right hand; but it shall not come near you. Only with your eyes shall you look, and see the reward of the wicked.

Because you have made the LORD, who is my refuge, Even the Most High, your dwelling place, No evil shall befall you, Nor shall any plague come near your dwelling; For He shall give His angels charge over you, to keep you in all your ways. In their hands they shall bear you up, lest you dash your foot against a stone. You shall tread upon the lion and the cobra, the young lion and the serpent you shall trample underfoot.

Because he has set his love upon me, therefore I will deliver him; I will set him on high, because he has known My name. He shall call upon Me, and I will answer him; I will be with him in trouble; I will deliver him and honor him. With long life I will satisfy him, and show him My salvation." (NKJV)

For many years that Psalm has brought me hope and comfort, but never as it did the day I was confronted with life and death ministry. I so loved the precious Tanzanian people that one day I said to God, *"If I can't hug them and love them, I can't minister to them."* God knew exactly what I meant and I never caught anything from the Tanzanian people—no AIDS, no scabies, no ringworm, no lice. Love conquers all. There were many times when the Lord answered our prayers for the healing of His people, and there were times when we did not receive the answers we sought. Nevertheless, God never ceased to be loving, merciful, righteous, or faithful.

Faithful and True

The Lord is faithful... he will strengthen and protect you from the evil one. (2 Thess. 3:3 NIV)

Trusting in God's love and really believing all things work together for the good of those that love Him was a real issue after the Patandi Village debacle. It just didn't seem as if anything good could come of such a mess. Even our faithful Maasai worker Longida had begun to have doubts—only his were about us! Was God really with them? The enemy was surely attacking his mind to cast doubt about us in order to try to divide us—as the Word says, *a house divided cannot stand.* He was such a young man not yet experienced in the challenges involved in groundbreaking Gospel ministry. One day shortly after the move he prayed and asked God, "Are you with them?" God opened Longida's eyes to behold the angelic hosts guarding our compound. God had confirmed He was with us, *for the Lord will vindicate his people and have compassion on his servants.* (Psalm 135:14 NIV) Scriptures make it clear that angels are a reality, and that Jesus is the Captain of the Hosts. Daily we looked to God for His protection! Asking the Lord to send His guardian angels was part of our personal daily arsenal against the enemy.

Are not all angels ministering spirits sent to serve those who will inherit salvation? (Heb. 1:14 NIV)

Life was indeed stressful after the emergency move. My total recovery was slow in coming. And the devilish scheme was not completed as some weeks later after having been safely relocated to Moshi, I received the dreadful news that our former Patandi gardener had just died of a hemorrhagic fever. I was overcome with grief. I began dwelling on all the horrible things that had happened in the village: the bleeding death of our German shepherd dogs from poisoning, my issue of blood, and now the young man whose life was just snuffed out. Rather than recounting God's guidance and faithfulness toward us, now distraught, I began to question God's love for me.

At that very second, for no natural reason, a Christian plaque hanging on the wall of our new Moshi home crashed violently to the floor. Startled, it grabbed my attention! I read these words: *I asked Jesus, "How much do You love me?" "This much,"* *He answered and He stretched our His arms and died.* Broken, I fell onto the cement and sobbed in repentance for ever having doubted God's love and faithfulness in guiding our lives. Once again an angel miraculously intervened when the devil was trying to bring doubt about my Father's love and turn my wounded heart against Him. *Finally, brethren, whatever things are true, whatever things are noble, whatever things are just, whatever things are pure, whatever things are lovely, whatever things are of good report, if there is any virtue and if there is anything praiseworthy—**meditate on these things**..., and the God of peace will be with you.* (Phil. 4:8-9 NKJV)

No matter how dire the circumstances, I needed to remember Jesus' promise that He would "never leave me nor forsake me." God's word is settled in heaven and His truth needed to override every lie of the enemy. Taking my eyes off Jesus, the author and finisher of my faith was a certain pathway to despondency and despair and could eventually lead to spiritual depression. Had God not sent the men from Nguruma village church to watch and pray for two nights? Had not Mike Rothery showed up with the announcement to get out now, and then stayed to help us move? Had not God opened Longida's eyes to see the holy angels encamped about our home? Surely the faithfulness of the Lord endures forever.

The attack of the enemy upon us and our ministry had not ended yet. This time it was waged against Terry. Shortly after the end of the Bible school term that same month, Terry had a huge thorn puncture the thick sole of his tennis shoes, penetrating his flesh and hitting the bone of his foot. As a precautionary measure, we had started him on antibiotics immediately; we became very concerned when a red line started up his leg. The red line warning screamed at us that the antibiotics were not working. Again despair was trying to raise its ugly head as we had been through so much in the last couple months that we were almost too weak to fight anymore. Anyone who ever read the *Snows of Kilimanjaro* by Hemingway knows the result of thorn infection can be lethal.

We were laying there helpless on our stark wood frame African bed with the typical six inch foam mattress. We had been in total anxiety of heart not knowing what to do. We continued to cry out to God and finally put it in His hands and gave up. We had actually started laughing at what a pitiful sight we must have been! Both of us were laid out on the bed—me with my back in agony from the horrific roads, and him with the thorn infection—when suddenly there was an unexpected honk at the gate. We could hear our Maasai guard, Yohanna, rush to unlock the gate his bows and arrows rattling and the jingle of the sword at his side. Because Yohanna greeted them so robustly, we were sure it was someone we all knew. I got up slowly trying not to strain my back and went to unlock the kitchen door and the grill work to greet the visitors. An unfamiliar truck appeared around the far corner of the house and parked in the driveway. It was Anne with a strange man. That night a physician, who had recently completed a course in tropical diseases, and was returning to Tanzania to minister to the people was staying in the Streets' home. Having told him our situation, the doctor came right over and told us we needed to add metronidazole tablets to the antibiotics prescribed. Fortunately they were in the house as we always used them for giardiasis and amoeba infections—both common after any trip to minister. Recently it had been discovered that puncture wounds in third world countries were requiring such meds to conquer any possible anaerobic bacteria in the wound. The next day we saw great improvement and by the end of the second day the line had disappeared. Again and again God showed Himself faithful to preserve our lives. What started out as another life or death situation became one more opportunity for our God of miracles to be glorified. In Psalm 68 verse 20 we read: *Our God is the God of salvation; and to GOD the Lord belong escapes from death.* (NKJV)

Some months later we learned that the curse of blood had not yet ended. Our evil landlord's son bled to death from a knife wound received during a barroom brawl. Bleeding from the stab wound, he tragically died in the dirt by the entry gate of our former Patandi property.

A curse of blood had been put on that property; all the deaths were hemorrhage related. But with God's help my bleeding stopped, I ... *overcame him* (the devil) *by the blood of the Lamb and by the word of* my *testimony.* (Rev. 12:11 NKJV) After a powerful prayer in the name above all names, Jesus, soulish prayer had been defeated! Faithfully God had revealed the cause of my bleeding and taught me how to deal with it.

A seasoned missionary from Sierra Leone helped me to understand the principle—that a curse put on God's people would eventually return to the one who sent it. *Like a flitting sparrow, like a flying swallow, so a curse without cause shall not alight.* (Prov. 26:2) Many years of ministry experience in Sierra Leone had taught her the things she now taught me about the workings of witchcraft in the spiritual realm.

Years later, at a conference in Dar-es-Salaam, the Holy Spirit revealed to me there was a woman with an issue of blood in the meeting. Giving a brief testimony of my personal struggle, I again prayed the prayer of faith breaking all the power of the soulish prayers against her. Instantly, she, too, was miraculously healed. Sunday she testified in church giving glory to God!

Witchdoctors and curses are woven into African culture. A person motivated by an evil desire such as greed or lust could go to the witchdoctor. A deal would then be struck and the curse would be placed on something or someone. Without the knowledge of God's power to cancel the curse, a villager could fall into such fear that the curse could manifest its wickedness—sometimes leading to death. By demonic power, circumstances were manipulated to enact the wicked person's will. In the case of our landlord, he would charge the tenant rent for a year in advance. Then through the power of evil he made the tenants life so miserable that they would leave his compound early—without a refund. But his greed ended in horrific tragedy; it cost him his son's life. Had the sins of the father passed to the son?

We had witnessed spiritual warfare beyond anything we ever imagined, but no matter what the devil sent our way God won! One day using His creation the Lord God powerfully illustrated this for us. It was the rainy season. As so often happens during an electrical storm, the power had failed. Because power failure was such a frequent occurrence, on the left side of our refrigerator we would keep an eight-inch strip of duct tape. Whenever the electricity clicked off, we would immediately wrap that sticky gray tape across the refrigerator door to stop anyone from opening it and releasing the cold air now trapped inside. That way food could be preserved for at least a day.

It had been a stress-filled day. Before the power went out, we were already annoyed about some incident involving an errant pastor who refused to repent and was causing many problems in the village by the Bible school. The enemy was on the attack again. Every time we thought the situation was over, the man would throw us another curve; we were exasperated! What to do next? Eat!

Cooking was impossible due to the power outage. We were as hungry as we were disgusted by the situation. Deciding to do something special to take our minds off the craziness, Terry went to the newly opened Chinese restaurant for takeout. We were thrilled the Chinese came to town. Another familiar *American* thing!

By the time Terry returned the rain had ceased, but the power had not returned. We decided to eat outside on the picnic table since the house was getting dark inside. Suddenly, as we sat there just casually munching on our delicious Chinese take-out, a drama was unfolding before our eyes. The sky had begun to fill with flying termites set free by the heavy rains. First, some really large termites swarmed. From nowhere, two majestic eagles appeared. Taking turns, they would dive, grasp a termite in their talons, and then gracefully pull it up to their mouths. They munched as if they were eating corn on the cob. That continued until all the large size termites were devoured. Next mid-sized termites, wings flapping wildly, filled the air. At least a dozen Weaver birds, known for weaving intricately designed nests of many varieties, came, attacked, and ate their fill. When that swarm ended, little termites came; along with them came little birds like the purple finch and pink cheeked vireo. We watched spellbound as the feasting continued until not one flying termite survived. What a feast we were all having as God taught us a great spiritual lesson about order in His universe.

The Holy Spirit used that dramatic sign in the sky to teach us something about the battle which ensues between God's holy angels and the forces of darkness. Whatever scheme the prince of darkness threw at us, God and His angelic army is bigger and more powerful than every destructive plan of the enemy. *The* LORD *is faithful, and he will strengthen and protect you from the evil one.* (2 Thess. 3:3 NIV) God's angelic hosts were on duty, ready to be dispatched to deal with any attack. No assignment of Satan could possibly ever be greater than the power of God to overcome. We were in the care of a faithful, loving Heavenly Father who never slumbers nor sleeps. The prayers of God's people around the world continually hedged us in.

*The angel of the L*ORD *encamps around those who fear him, and he delivers them.* (Ps. 34:7 NIV)

*Praise the L*ORD, *you his angels, you mighty ones who do his bidding, who obey his word. Praise the L*ORD, *all his heavenly hosts, you his servants who do his will.* (Ps.103:20-22 NIV)

As we prayed God would send the angels—even as He promised! Indeed the Lord is faithful and true to perform His word! *The LORD will perfect that which concerns me.* (Ps. 138:8 NKJV)

Our new town Moshi had become and would truly continue to be a place of refuge during the eventful days and years ahead. Each day was different and each contained a lesson for us in God's school. Again and again we learned—no matter the problem God was BIGGER!

City of Refuge: The Town of Moshi

For financial reasons, we had moved from Arusha to Patandi Village, where we literally escaped with our lives. Our new residence would be in Shanty Town, a small community outside city center of Moshi. For the remainder of our years in Tanzania, we would call Moshi home. The town is located in the lowlands at the base of Mount Kilimanjaro. According to the 2002 census, Moshi had a population of 144,739. The home was designed with two separate bedroom wings. Brian moved into the wing opposite ours. His joyful presence helped to settle our hearts after the Patandi village tragedy. We missed our sons so much, and having Brian now living in Moshi was a blessing beyond comprehension. The timing was right, as we were about to go on furlough. Continued occupancy of a compound was always a great deterrent to the constant nightly threat of thievery. Later he told us that as we pulled out of the driveway, he said to the workers, *"There will not be a word of English spoken on this compound until Mom and Dad return."*

Shortly after we returned from furlough, we returned with Brian to Manyara for a baptismal celebration service. It had been six months since we showed the *Jesus Film*. Thirty of the men, women, and youth who had given their lives to Jesus the previous November were prepared to make a public confession of faith through baptism. It was an important step in the lives of these new believers. Baptism was a loud public event that drew a huge crowd informing everyone of the new Christian's stand for Christ! As the church members walked to the river, it became a colorful two kilometer Gospel music parade. Drums beat, saints sang, and villagers joined the throng as they all walked along joyfully singing God's praises. Taking advantage of the opportunity, Terry then preached the Gospel of salvation by faith in Jesus. Touched by the message, three additional villagers came forward and asked if they could be saved and baptized right then with the others. It was a Book of Acts experience, not unlike when Philip met the Ethiopian eunuch. *They came to some water and the eunuch said, "Look, here is water. Why shouldn't I be baptized?"* (Acts 8:36 NIV)

It was a very warm, sunny morning. Prior to our arrival at the river, a group of about twelve preadolescent boys had gathered on the opposite bank of the river to swim. They had disrobed before we arrived and were about to jump in when they heard us coming. Feeling very embarrassed about their nakedness, they each grabbed a single stemmed leaf cluster and placed it between their legs as they sat quietly on the bank. Respectfully the boys sat listening. I could tell a couple of them were touched by the message but held back from responding. Sadly, they looked to the left and to the right trying to see how the others would respond. As soon as the last person was baptized and the final "amen" was sounded, off came the leaves, each boy plunging head first into the cool river waters below. That was the glorious beginning of a four-day evangelistic tour. One night we showed a video about witchcraft called *The Charm*. Twenty-four adult men, both Maasai and Iraqw, gave their lives to Jesus. Village decisions rested with the elders; leadership in salvation opened the way for the women and children to freely receive Jesus. It was a *kairos* moment for the village.

Our visits helped to encourage our students and build up the body of Christ. It was during the last term of the Moshi Bible school that the pastor from Manyara, Ndelio Nanyaro, testified that he was about to quit the ministry—until God touched him, with the Holy Spirit filling him afresh. At his church the next morning, Brian preached and four more received Jesus as Savior. After the service we continued our drive up the ridge to the Ngorongoro plateau to visit the church of another Bible school student. There I preached on *Hope Eternal* and seventeen more prayed to receive Jesus, or so I thought. Later, in talking with the pastor, Brian found out that many of them were already Christians, but didn't want the *mzungu* preacher to feel bad, so they came forward again. Another lesson learned: pray for authentic converts—not *mzungu* pleasers! After dark we showed the *Jesus Film* again and seven more adult men plus many others committed their lives to the Lord. For a man to humble himself before the crowd and acknowledge his need for a Savior was a bold societal move. God was on the move in the region. Hearts were being challenged and changed by the Holy Spirit.

We were on the move again on Monday to show the *Jesus Film* at Pastor James Sirikwa's church in the Karatu area. It was the first time I would meet his wife, Dorcas. She was a lively, cheerful woman with great zeal for God. Later I would know that was a divine appointment, for her destiny was entwined in ours.

The crowd was not as large as usual, since it was a sparsely populated, dry, desolate area. Nevertheless, over one hundred twenty responded to the invitation to pray to receive Christ.

We were rejoicing in God's goodness when James came to inform us that he had a miracle to share with us. During the last term of the Moshi Bible School when the Holy Spirit had visited us mightily, God had a word for Pastor James that he was going to have a miracle. It was with great joy that we were introduced to his miracle. A precious young woman came forth. For sixteen years she had been possessed by a demon. When Pastor James prayed for her, she was delivered and set free. Jesus said in Luke 10:19, *"Behold, I give you the authority to trample on serpents and scorpions, and over all the power of the enemy."* (NKJV) Later she was able to return to public school and complete her education. A true miracle indeed!

And He (Jesus) said to them, *"Go into all the world and preach the gospel to every creature. He who believes and is baptized will be saved; but he who does not believe will be condemned. And these signs will follow those who believe: In My name they will cast out demons."* (Mark 16:15-17 NKJV)

Whether in distant villages or in the town of Moshi, horrific issues plagued the people of Tanzania with much suffering. Orphans from the AIDS epidemic, starvation, disease, and peril more than I could imagine were everywhere. The beauty of the majestic mountain in the near distance was a constant contrast between the innumerable possible horrors of everyday life including the village lepers lining the streets raising swollen, infected, fingerless hands begging for food.

Whenever we would visit our post office box near city center, we would pass a leper woman positioned there. Both of us felt great compassion for the helpless victims of Hansen's disease;

regularly we would give money to the woman positioned by our post box. To her we had become a faithful source of support and a relationship ensued. One particular day Terry had blessed her abundantly. Her gratitude exceeded our gift. She was so blessed that in raising her hand to say *"Asante sana,"* (thank you very much) she touched Terry's hand. As fast as possible, my fear-gripped microbiologist husband sped home rumbling into the compound with dust flying for a good hand washing of *Jik* (a bleach product). Hearing him arrive, I was startled at his speed, for we often joked that I operate in high gear and he almost in reverse. He was accelerating on that day!

One of the blessings of residing near the highlands on Mount Kilimanjaro and Meru was the abundance of fresh food products. The areas were extremely productive agricultural lands flourishing with coffee, banana trees, and vegetables. But as the land descended water resources diminished, and the closer to the areas of the savannah lands, the more critical the situation and the more the people suffered drought conditions. Most village Tanzanian families are largely sustained by the agrarian culture and are dependent upon the seasonal rains for their crops. The rains were becoming more and more unpredictable and undependable. Season after season we grieved with the people as we all watched their maize crop wither due to insufficient rains and the heat of the merciless African sun.

Land in Tanzania is collectively owned by extended clans. The land is then subdivided into individual family-owned plots. At the death of the father, the land was divided equally among the sons. That principle of division only works well for a few generations. A piece of pie can only be cut into so many pieces. The later generations' ability to produce enough maize on a miniscule piece of property contributed to the family's struggle for survival. Extended family groups are tightly knitted. Territorial closeness provides protection as well as the necessary emotional support. In Tanzania, the entire village nurtures the children and cares for older adults. Children are raised by *mama mdogo*, the mother's younger sister, and *mama mkubwa*, mother's older sister. All family women share in the responsibility for the well-being and care of the children. Relationships are a top priority to them.

Traditionally, another major task for the women was farming the land; although the men inherited the land, the women worked it. If they were fortunate, they had a *jembe* (hoe), if none, planting was done using a stick and/or by hand. Village women were destined to a life of total drudgery: farming; carrying water—usually very long distances; building the house; birthing and caring for the children; caring for any animals; clothes washing; shopping; sweeping the perimeter of the house even though it was surrounded by dirt; and everything else that needed to be done. A major portion of a woman's day involved meal preparation using either firewood or charcoal. The huge consumption of wood was adding to the increasingly erratic seasonal rains. The greater the deforestation for necessary firewood, charcoal production, or frame house construction, the worse the rain situation became—and the more desolate the land and the hungrier the people! Famine relief would eventually become part of our missionary outreach.

The suffering of the people in general was at times overwhelming. My heart was especially broken for the conditions of the Maasai women. Daily they traveled long distance for water. Kilometer after kilometer they walked with huge yellow barrel-shaped containers of water, one on their heads and perhaps another in their hands; sometimes they might even use a donkey for hauling the heavy water containers—but I never saw a woman riding one. It just wasn't done! Everywhere they went, they plodded along in black sandals made of tire treads or colorful flip flops. Their colorful blue clothing and magnificent complex beaded jewelry decorated them from head down to their ankles and set them apart as unique—but they were second class citizens.

In Maasai culture, cattle represent wealth. Maasai men value their livestock far above their wives. A Maasai man was questioned about his decision to get medicine for his sick cow rather than for his sick spouse. The man was overheard saying he could always get another wife. Add to that the fact that many tribes, especially the Maasai, continued the rite of passage including female circumcision. It is an abhorrent practice, killing some and maiming many each year. In the last two decades, it has become a devilish procedure spreading the AIDS virus among both the young women and the young men. Typically the same instrument is used on a number of women, and it is easily contaminated. Many have asked, "What we have done to stop it?" Eventually after some training in Kenya, I taught about AIDS. Information is one thing; heart transformation is another. The honest answer I give to someone inquiring about this tragedy, "God has instructed me to preach the Gospel as only Jesus can change hearts, and only changed hearts change culture!" A society that honors the Bible lives by the truths of the Bible. Our job was to teach the truth that sets the captives free wherever we found them. What an enormous job we had to do!

There were three kinds of hunger in the land: emotional, physical, and spiritual. God had granted us great favor with the Moshi community and had opened the door for an amazing ministry our first year in Moshi. There were children whose parents had died of AIDS or who had simply been abandoned to live on the streets. Survival drives them to steal or beg or both. Local orphanages do what they can, but often the unattended children become addicted to glue and prefer the independence and freedom of the street environment. After moving to Moshi, we began noticing preteen boys coming to the Bible school campus and begging for food. We soon discovered that they were part of an orphanage that had been abandoned when a former missionary had suddenly departed. Virtually all their funding except for what we were able to give them had been discontinued. Most of the boys had run away back to the street because it was better than the home. The children were destitute. Our hearts were deeply touched by their plight, and we began helping them with food, soap, and other personal hygiene items. As a result, some of the boys returned from the streets to the home. There were nine boys settled at the orphanage, which was located just a few hundred yards from where we taught our Bible classes. During the school sessions, we brought them over to eat at the Bible school. How could we not live what we taught?

But be doers of the word, and not hearers only...Pure and undefiled religion before God and the Father is this: to visit orphans and widows in their trouble, and to keep oneself unspotted from the world. (James 1:22 NKJV)

One of the greatest challenges of being a missionary is finding and sticking to God's purpose for you in the foreign land. Needs are everywhere! We were only two people and we could only do so much. Money only went so far! We tried to encourage the boys and bless them whenever possible, but our main goal was to minister to the whole person, and that included sharing God's love and the promise of life eternal through His Son, Jesus. So occasionally Longida and I would go down to visit the orphanage and try to do a Bible study with them. One day, being without transportation, we walked from home to a main road to await a bus. That broken tarmac/dirt road was usually busy with buses as it was the road to KCMC, the local Lutheran Hospital. It was very hot and no buses were coming by. An old dilapidated pickup truck was coming close. Boldly I put out my hand and flipped my palm up and down in the "give me a lift" signal commonly used by the locals. He stopped. I jumped in the back as Longida, his mouth wide open, joined me. We bounced our way to town and departed our lift only after surrendering our bus fare to the truck driver. Another lesson learned: no free rides for *mzungu!*

Although fun, my teaching the boys was really a disaster. My Swahili was poor and Longida's English not much better, so his translating for me was next to impossible. Eventually we decided it would be better if he were to go minister the Bible study on his own. It was the beginning of God's call on his life to one day become a Maasai pastor. Until we found another missionary to take over the ministry, he was faithful to minister to their spirits as we continued to nurture their bodies. Jesus said it like this: *"Assuredly, I say to you, inasmuch as you did it to one of the least of these My brethren, you did it to Me."* (Matthew 25:40 NKJV) Loving those beautiful street boys was a natural for us as God had given us two wonderful sons. When Christmas came, we were excited to bless them in abundance. Shopping for them had released afresh the joyous spirit of Christmas within me. Each boy received a Bible and his own bag overflowing with presents. The orphans erupted with joy as they opened shirts, combs, pencils, pens, ball caps, and cookies. On went the ball caps. Joy unspeakable erupted as they squealed and jumped around. One little fella picked up his package of cookies and licked the outside wrapper. Even the anticipation of the sugary treat excited him. They were overwhelmed with God's love for them. Most had probably never received any gift. Christmas presented for us the opportunity to represent Jesus and His love to them. It was truly a cup of cold water given in Jesus' name, because hundreds of supporters had given sacrificially to us. What an unforgettable December 24th it was for them and us.

The day was already full of glory and another amazing God-ordained event was yet to occur. Never shall I forget that Christmas Eve. Anita Leaman, an Elim missionary from Pennsylvania, had joined us for the holiday. Brian, Anita, Terry, and I, along with Benji Street, went to a juvenile detention center. It was a minimum security jail for teens located in Moshi. One young child was detained because out of desperate hunger he had stolen a handful of peanuts from a neighbor.

Justice is demanded and mercy is rare when people live such desperate lives. Heartbreak is everywhere, but that night God's mercy prevailed.

For the most part, foreigners are forbidden to enter secure government facilities such as this. Truly a Christmas miracle—permission to show the *Jesus Film* in a typically off-limits youth detention center, on this, the holiest of nights! We arrived with great anticipation of what God was about to do. Exiting the car, I cringed as the smell of rotted garbage and the stench of an open running sewer filled my nostrils. It was only God's grace that kept me from turning and running. God had a mission and no assignment or discouragement from the enemy would prevail. We were there to show the *Jesus Film* to several workers and fifteen boys. As we entered what must have been their dining hall, we noticed tables and chairs were lined up and they were ready to receive us. We were so grateful to God that night for electricity. The power was on both in Moshi and in heaven. At the conclusion of the film, all the workers and fourteen of those fifteen boys responded to the greatest of all Christmas gifts, Jesus, and the Father's promise of life eternal. Humbly hardened detention guards and broken delinquent boys bowed their heads and prayed to ask Jesus into their hearts and lives. It was indeed a holy night. *For God so loved the world (forgotten children) that He gave His only begotten Son, that whoever believes in Him should not perish but have everlasting life. For God did not send His Son into the world to condemn the world, but that the world through Him might be saved.* (John 3:16-17 NKJV) The next day, December 25th, held another first for us. Living in western New York in close proximity to a spiritualist community, we thought we had learned a lot about spiritual warfare. But nothing completely prepared us for the onslaught of the demonic activity that we experienced in Africa. Christmas Day began with worship and prayer. Later, the four of us went off to the Streets' for a lovely meal. Sharing the British traditions of funny hats and party poppers filled with surprises was such fun. However, when we returned home there were sulfurous odors in our house and a strange feeling of extreme tension. We had confusion, no peace of spirit, and our dog, Baraka, was going berserk. After much authoritative warfare prayer in Jesus' name, we were delivered from this attack.

Weeks later we learned that the neighboring Kilimanjaro tribe, the Chaggas, had a wicked December 25th tradition. Yearly all the tribal family members gathered together during the Christmas holiday to perform sacrifices and worship ancestral spirits to release the ancestors blessings upon their lives for the coming year—more wealth to themselves. Our house was owned by a Kilimanjaro Chagga. We were beginning to understand the powerful links between generations. Moshi is located in the heart of Chagga land; we were challenged to understand the traditions of the Chagga tribe. On the surface they seemed to be church-going, prosperous, business-minded people, but if that prosperity was somehow linked to witchcraft, we missionaries had more work to do.

Like most tribes, the Chagga are steeped in many traditions. The mountains isolate them and preserve their traditions. Much to the chagrin of their elders, the younger generation is adopting western clothing styles due to the increase in safari tourism in Moshi and Arusha. Within the Chagga tribe, a daughter wearing slacks brings shame and dishonor to her father. Among the older Christians, whether in the village or the city, a snug short skirt or slacks of any kind are considered unacceptable attire. The reason is simply that in areas such as the rural Tanzanian mountain villages, Muslim communities along the East African coast, or on the Maasai plains, women wearing slacks are usually considered to be prostitutes.

Thus, clothing is an issue that can be difficult to handle for foreigners or visitors. Great offense can be taken when there is insensitivity to cultural practices which can result in unproductive ministry. Those bound in religious traditions are often the hardest to reach. First there is the women issue, but added to that perhaps is what possible value could there be to anything a woman of the evening, one wearing slacks, had to share? Gospel warriors are called to go and make disciples. That challenge can be significant even in the area of dress. Successful village ministry meant adapting to the acceptable local culture. Jesus said, *Thou shalt love thy neighbour as thyself.* (Matt. 22:39 KJV) Loving others is not always comfortable, nor is it convenient! But disciples must follow their Master who came to serve and not be served. No questions asked! Paul had a few words concerning putting up with difficult circumstances, *Therefore I endure all things for the elect's sakes, that they may also obtain the salvation which is in Christ Jesus with eternal glory.* (2 Tim. 2:10 NKJV) Unselfishly abiding by cultural standards (unless sinful) is certainly obeying the words of Jesus to love one's neighbor.

We loved the people of Moshi and when they laughed we laughed and when they grieved we also grieved. As international women, we met together on Wednesdays on Anne Street's porch where we found love and fellowship with women from all over Europe, Asia, America, Canada, India, and many African nations. We were women of many faiths, but we studied the Bible together and prayed to Jesus. We lived in peace with our neighbors most of the year. Our Muslim grocer and later the Muslim baker would greet us by name. It was a friendly, secure town with no signs of religious tension. Peace and love flowed freely one to another.

Then 9/11 happened! After the attack on America, the attitudes of many Muslim shopkeepers drastically changed toward Americans. The city's atmosphere was laden with caution and suspicion. Relationships radically changed, when in actuality none of us had personally changed. Suddenly, unexpectedly, we were in some silent war with one another. Islam was aggressively attempting to evangelize the town. When we first moved to Moshi, there was one mosque situated in the small village of Longoni about thirty minutes drive from town center. It was heartbreaking for us to pass the local Muslim men dressed in their white *shukas*. Their joyless faces reflected the intense hardness of their hearts toward us and the Gospel. Neither they nor the spirit ruling them wanted our presence or our life-giving message. They had an agenda; Christianity had no part in it!

First the village imam began giving out water to the local Longoni people. Then, in full view of the community, he began teaching the children to read from the Koran. There were local schools, but education was expensive. Most families sent only the firstborn son to school, and then only up to the equivalent of our seventh grade. Not only were all the village children being proselytized by the reading program, but other mosques were rapidly being built. By the time we left Moshi, the loud call to prayer could be heard from four mosques in the vicinity of the Bible school. As Arab oil money saturated the area, mosques were popping up not only in Moshi, but all along the bus line to Arusha.

The various buses were major people movers. Larger coaches traveled the long distance runs to major cities and other countries. Most village people's mode of transportation was primarily by foot—and often barefoot. Flip flops were sometimes saved for visits to town. Those with a job could sometimes afford a bicycle, but no matter the means, people seemed to be always on the move. Locally *matatus* (mini buses) *ruled* the road! At the bus stands and throughout the villages, bus barkers clamored for business. These local people movers had a seating capacity for about seventeen passengers, but that never stopped the locals from doubling maximum capacity by crowding onto others' laps or hanging onto the windows or bumpers with their bodies pressed against the sides of the bus as they sped along. Those mini buses were a recipe for disaster. Periodically tragedy would strike, killing and maiming many. With emotions running high, the bus driver, if still alive, would climb out from the bus and quickly flee—disappearing for fear of his life. It was not uncommon for an angry mob to attempt to stone him to death. In Kenya, I once saw a cartoon of a rambling *matatu* with puffs of dust billowing from beneath its speeding wheels and a fierce expression on the front end. The headlights, as the eyes, were wild with madness and the teeth-like grillwork was shaped into a menacing frown. The caption read, *"Kenya's weapons of mass destruction."* An East African bus had the potential for being a death trap due to lack of maintenance, impossible roads, and the dangerous, fatalistic attitudes of the Muslim *matatu* drivers, who passed on blind curves, stating if it's Allah's will we will pass successfully. The region was so in need of God's wisdom and grace. Thankfully our Bible school was in place to help with the transformation of our region and beyond.

Moshi Bible School: A Light in the Darkness

According to Jeremiah 29:11, God has a divine plan and purpose for each one of us. From 1997 until 2001 until we moved to Nairobi, Kenya, God's plan for us was to teach Tanzanian Christian leaders and facilitate the operation of the Moshi PEFA Bible School.

The vision cast for the Moshi Bible School was a thorough Bible education while preserving the students working relationships within their local churches. Terms ran for three weeks, three times a year for four years, ending with a Bible diploma. Each course was one week in length. By the end of the term the students had each completed three courses. The course rotation was consistent, making it possible for students to enter during any term and finish exactly four years later. Limiting the Bible school term to three weeks facilitated keeping the pastoral students in touch with their local churches. After only two Sundays away, they returned home with fresh fire and new insights ready to be imparted to their congregation. It was a powerful ministry of multiplication! The entire body of Christ benefitted as together the pastor and his flock grew spiritually. And most importantly, the pastor was able to maintain his role as their shepherd.

"Faculty meetings" consisted of Terry coming into my home office and asking me, "What course would you like to teach?" In the beginning there were only two of us on staff at our Bible school. Originally, the curriculum was modeled after Elim Bible Institute, Lima, NY. Each term Terry taught an Old Testament course and I taught either theology or New

Testament. The third lecturer was usually an anointed guest speaker—men such as Pastor Andy Zack, Pastor Chris Lonneville, Pastor John Wentworth, Dr. Lee Simmons, and our son, Brian, who pastored a local church in Moshi. We felt impressed by the Holy Spirit to provide detailed course books for the students to facilitate classroom instruction and a home reference library. Course books were prepared by each teacher and then translated into Swahili by Lazaro Kiriama. Amazingly, our second Sunday in Tanzania we met Pastor Kiriama, the man who would enable us to make that happen; eventually he would become Terry's "Timitheo" (Timothy). Before we knew how desperately we would need him, God's divine guidance brought him into our lives!

After church we visited the Kiriamas' home, where over a cup of tea, God began to knit our hearts together. Eventually Pastor Lazaro Kiriama, a Maasai from the Arusha region, became our full-time translator. The spirit of excellence was upon him; he was a brilliant man with an MS degree who had schooled both in the USA and UK. His mastery of the American English language made him the perfect resource for the high quality of translation required for our Bible school materials. Later we knew that one day this dynamic Christian leader would become the principal of the school now known as Kilimanjaro Christian College.

Before all that could transpire, God had a lot of arranging and rearranging to do to establish that part of His work through us in Tanzania. After Pastor Chris and Paul Shultz revealed to us the questionable behavior they observed in the college campus pastor, we approached the area overseer with the proof of his

152

ungodly behavior. The overseer's response about the incidents was to ask if their American church was a big giver. To us that was irrelevant, but to them money moved mountains. Eventually the PEFA elders agreed it was time to remove him as the campus pastor. In Tanzanian culture, shame is such an issue that dealing with sin was almost impossible for them. If American supporters had not witnessed his negative behaviors, he might still be the campus pastor today.

Instead of setting the former pastor aside for a season of discipline and restoration, the PEFA elders decided to give him yet another chance. He was to move to his home village and begin afresh by planting a church there. Having agreed to follow their direction, he came to us requesting the money necessary to rent a truck and hire men to help him with his move. When Terry asked how much was needed, as it was a long way, the response was fifty thousand shillings or about forty dollars. Grateful for a solution to what had been a real headache for us both, Terry gave him the money. Finally, it was over! Unfortunately, by the next weekend, he had not moved to the mountain, but literally around the corner from the Bible school, where he started a church in his home and began badmouthing the college and us throughout the neighborhood.

Shortly after his departure from campus, we got an outlandish bill from the electric company. Each month during the past year, Terry had faithfully given money to the former pastor to pay the electric bill for the compound. We soon discovered that not only had he pocketed the money, he had also run electric wires to surrounding houses from the campus and was charging them a fee. He had become the Langoni electric company at our expense. The bill was well over one thousand USD.

After prayer we felt the Lord reveal to us it was His will to invite the Kiriama family to pastor the Langoni PEFA Church and to work alongside of us at the Bible school. When we approached them with the idea of moving from their home in beautiful green Moivaro, a village outside of Arusha, to the Bible school compound house, there was understandably some resistance. For them it meant leaving their family, friends, and family lands in a cool climate with a plentiful supply of river water to move to the dust bowl at the Bible school. One day the Lord changed Eli's heart as she prayed. Before her was a vision of all that we and our family had sacrificed to come to minister to the people of Tanzania—our home, our family, our friends. Telling me this, her face filled with emotion as she said, "How can we do any less for our own countrymen?" Early on I challenged her to attend the school and to become the first pastor's wife to graduate. The success or failure of God's plan to elevate the women from cultural bondages to freedom in Christ rested upon her willingness to accept the call, take the challenge, and be in place as God parted the waters of the cultural divide. Eli visibly working alongside Lazaro on campus was critical for the advancement of any Tanzanian husband/wife ministry team approach. She had three boys at home at the time, so balancing home, family and church was not an easy thing for her, but she consented. Eli's godly example spoke quiet volumes for the future advancement of other pastors' wives. Within a couple years as an outstanding graduate of the Moshi Bible School, Eli became the dean of women of the anointed school which became Kilimanjaro

Christian College. Copying our leadership model, Lazaro and Eli became powerful examples for all of the PEFA leadership of a husband/wife team cooperating and working together as Gospel warriors. To this day, their servant leadership continues to guide the church and college in Moshi. Additionally, Eli now leads the national PEFA women, and Lazaro is the overseer in Kilimanjaro District.

After God had confirmed they were to move to Moshi and partner together with us in the further establishment of the school for God's glory, with joyful hearts they moved into their new home which we remodeled to fit their family's needs. Eli took on the task of transforming the dust bowl campus into a beautiful garden. Eli had what the Tanzanians called "green fingers." The Bible college campus became alive with colorful shrubs, grass, shade trees, and various flowering plants.

A holy habitation for Jesus was being built. As we all continued to press into God for direction, the next term all night prayer was initiated with students praying in shifts of fifteen minutes throughout the night. Before long they came to ask, "Could we please pray for one hour?" In this holy place they met with their God. Truly Jesus was now Lord in that place!

The campus was now equipped with a church, a kitchen, and a beautiful multi-purpose building; it was large, bright, and airy and could be used as both a lecture hall and a dining hall. God had done a new thing bringing us the beautiful new building, and with the new wineskin came an atmosphere of holiness. The building and the team helped transform the campus. In August the project was completed when it was beautifully painted by our longtime friend, Alan Woodlee of Westfield, NY. The final touch was the hanging of a magnificent, Christ-honoring, purple and white banner declaring that "Jesus is Lord"—*"Yesu ni Bwana."* The banner made a declaration to everyone entering: Jesus was in charge in that place!

With the Kiriamas in position, we now had a team of four moving forward in the anointing of the Holy Spirit. Terry was the school principal. As administrator, it meant he did everything from food purchasing, hiring village women to carry water, hiring the cooks, buying firewood— all while teaching his class. None of those tasks were simple. He would go to the kitchen and inquire as to the cooks needs, and they would give him a carefully prepared list. The trip to town was at least an hour and a half, with sixty minutes of that on totally jarring roads. One day while Terry was in town, the students had their *chai* (tea) break. As soon as he returned from his trip into town, the cooks came to Terry and announced they were now out of sugar. He needed to return to town and buy sugar. When he asked them why they didn't tell him earlier when he was going into town about their need for sugar, their answer was simply, "We didn't need it then!" Planning ahead was a BIG issue—one which continually tried our patience.

Another difficult situation involved the compound grounds. Every time we planted grass plugs to help eliminate the dust issue, one of the eager early bird students would be up before sunrise pulling it out. This happened more than a few times as new students would arrive. An early morning tradition in Tanzania is to sweep the dirt in order to tidy up the yard. Grass was thought to be a yard hazard; after all, snakes could hide there! And it certainly gets in the way of the homemade whisk brooms made specifically to *fagia* (sweep). One of our sanitary issues involved trying to help Mama Ima, the older cook, understand the importance of cleanliness in the kitchen. One afternoon, as I passed by I noticed her using the same cloth to wipe the food preparation table that she had just used to wipe the filthy kitchen floor. Local chickens ran freely throughout the compound and into the kitchen at whim and in Tanzania, every shoe is equivalent to a barnyard shoe. Animal feces and Giardia are everywhere, mixed into the dust. That truly grossed me out! The next day we introduced the cooks to the power of bleach, locally called *Jik,* and carefully instructed them as to its proper use. And we tried to make a clear designation about floor cloths and kitchen surface wiping up cloths for the chopping areas. Never could she understand all our fussiness about using that *Jik* stuff and those separate cleaning cloths.

The other cleanliness issue involved trying to get the more remote village students to confine their toilet activities to the *choo.* Some had never experienced one. A bush and a leaf were more than enough for the mountain people. One particular mountain man would just get up, leave class, and go outside and urinate behind our classroom building. In the beginning I would cringe as I heard him. Everyone else was totally unmoved by the event. It's just what you do—got to go, then go! Wherever and whenever—*hamna shida* (no problem!) Actually after having visited some village *vyoo* (plural for toilets), I understood—give me a bush any day!

Because the Holy Spirit was moving among us, the school grew rapidly. People were coming from across the nation to be part of what God was doing in Moshi. And it was all God! Neither of us had ever taken a missions course. So we prayed and did what God told us to do! Everything we did was done only after God made us know, *this is the way walk ye in it!* We had one guide and He was God. Our motto was, *Trust in the LORD with all thine heart; and lean not unto thine own understanding. In all thy ways acknowledge him, and he shall direct thy paths.* (Prov. 3:5-6 KJV)

Each Bible school term was different, but the one that met in July 1999 was special. Psalm 103 begins, *Bless the Lord, O my soul, and all that is within me, bless His Holy Name!* And that is exactly what we were doing at the Bible school when the Spirit fell in miraculous power on Friday, July 11. Originally the course was designed to be an intensive study of the Psalms. The Holy Spirit had a different plan. The Holy Spirit was directing the students to have a "personal psalm" experience. Each student was to create a song or a psalm and put it to music. Some formed groups. For two days the class sang their psalms. It was so exciting to witness the joy and enthusiasm as God had inspired their musical creativity. They had heard God's voice to them and had encountered the unction of the Holy Spirit in a glorious new way. Traditionally when the Maasai sing, they ceremonially jump. How moving to witness seven former Maasai warriors surrendered to the anointing of the Spirit now—jumping for Jesus! The Holy Spirit made it clear we were not to stop there, but to encourage the students to a deeper level of personal praise. Following prayer, Holy Spirit inspiration came that collectively, as a class, we were to develop a list of descriptors of God. Joshua, one of the Maasai warriors, got so excited when he learned that God is a Mighty

Warrior. It was an "aha" moment for him. He could now identify with God. Each one was to choose three of the words and sing a personal song to Jesus. As they began to sing the song of the Spirit from their soul, many magnified the Lord in a formerly unknown way. Healings broke out. Others experienced deliverances as never before. No one touched anyone. It happened as the *Moto wa Mungu* (fire of God) penetrated them.

They began to fall all over. Many cried out as they were delivered from pain and despair. God was moving as never before in the Bible school. The anointing was so strong. Next each wrote on paper those personal things that bound them; those things that only total surrender to the power of the Holy Spirit could conquer. Earlier that week we had had a teaching on the power of the *shofar* (Hebrew word for a trumpet made of an animal horn) to purify the air and release God's glory as the enemy is dispelled. After collecting the papers, the *shofar* was blown over them. The power of God was released upon the men and women. They spontaneously began to shout to the Lord as they believed Him for total victory. The papers were burned and the sweetest communion service followed. The students gave glorious testimonies of the healings, both physical and emotional, and the powerful deliverances they received. The Holy Spirit was among us; the news spread throughout the land.

By October the Moshi Bible School attendance had grown to fifty-seven men and women attending. With the highest attendance recorded, the college in Moshi was now the largest of the PEFA Bible Schools. At that point we were pushing the capacity of the facilities beyond comfortable limits. Miracles were happening. Two new totally uneducated female students testified how God miraculously taught them to read when they were given a Bible! Now with the ability to read, they were able to attend school for the first time.

Another was a miracle of multiplication. One of our students, Ndelelio Nanyaro, pastoring a church at Manyara reported that he had started a Bible school to train leaders in the area between Lake Manyara and the Ngorongoro Crater! He had become an answer to a frequent prayer that God would give us fruit that would reproduce fruit—a ministry of multiplication. Using our materials from the Moshi School, he was teaching 20 additional church leaders! Years later those men and women became the first graduates of the future Lake Manyara Christian College. Pastor Nanyaro was on fire! He had experienced the power of God upon one day when the Spirit directed me to go lay hands on his right shoulder. Giving glory to God, he testified that Jesus had healed a motorcycle injury from years ago.

Another powerful way we began to expand the school was taking a course each term to the Maasai. An extension of the Bible school met in Maasailand. It began with one course from a previous term at the Moshi Bible School translated into Kimaasai (the language of the Maasai). The course was taught in a remote cow manure and mud church pastored by one of the Maasai students in our Moshi school. Lazaro, although from the Warusha Maasai tribe was able to communicate with them. The course was taught completely in the Maasai language and they loved it! Twenty-eight pastors and church leaders (all Maasai) from four different denominations attended the course. They were so appreciative for the teaching in their language. Previously missionaries had used Kiswahili in outreaches to the Maasai. This was one more reason we thank God that He sent Pastor Lazaro to work with us.

To hear the Word taught in their own language was a first for them! During the week the elder of the village came to see what was going on. He was so moved to hear the Word in his own language that before the end of the week, he prayed to receive Jesus as Savior. He even began attending the church. God loves us to minister across denominations. All those pastoral students were so appreciative. With thankful hearts they wrote Terry and conferred upon him the honorary title of *Laiboni,* the name by which they refer to the spiritual leader of their clan. In their tribal religion, the *Laiboni* lives near the Oldonyo Lengai (Mountain of God), a smoking volcanic mountain near the Ngorongoro Crater.

Having been a university professor, Terry's desire was for the campus to become an authentic learning center. That meant expanding the compound to include a library, some office space, and a guest room. In August 2000 a team from the Syracuse, New York area led by John Wicks came to complete the project. John's son was so impacted by the things he saw God do that today he is in the ministry.

We usually tried to provide our teams with various ministry opportunities. They were stoked about doing an evangelistic outreach and showing the *Jesus Film.* The pastor had done a good job of advertising the cinema and by the time the team arrived people had already begun to gather. The men helped set everything up for the showing of the film, but the generator refused to cooperate. For about an hour the team and Terry worked feverishly. In spite of the best efforts of all the team members, the generator wouldn't run. Finally they all placed their hands on the generator and fervently prayed in the mighty name of Jesus. Faith arose! Terry pulled the cord and the generator hummed the rest of the night. Many Tanzanians and Americans were blessed to see the power of God released before and during the showing of the *Jesus Film.*

Before the building team left for America, we gathered in the library and dedicated the building to the Lord. The next month when the students returned, they rejoiced about the future possibility of a library all their own. And we rejoiced about having guest quarters that included a shower and western toilet.

After all the prayers of the teams and the 24/7 prayers of the students, God was not only moving on campus, but about to move in the neighborhood. The October term of the Bible school was packed to capacity with fifty-seven students present and thirty more on a waiting list. Men and women were now coming all the way from the southern border with Zambia, east from the coast region by Dar es Salaam, and west as far as the Serengeti. During prayer and fasting, God revealed the need for more intense spiritual warfare. Together we were to engage in warfare not only for our ministries and families, but also for repentance of national sins. Attached to the lecture hall walls were sheets of paper to be used as prayer guides for the students as they prayed in unity throughout the night. As the Lord gave revelation, we followed. Next we were led by the Holy Spirit to do a seven-day Jericho march around the village of Langoni where the college is located. Each day we began at 6:45 AM in order to complete the march by 7:30 when classes began. Except for periodic blasts of the shofar, we marched like an army around the village praying silently, tearing down strongholds and waging war in the heavenlies. Then on the seventh day, we began at sunrise (6:00 AM) and marched seven times around, finishing about noon. On the seventh time, God gave us a Holy Spirit anointed Swahili marching song. We marched proclaiming the mighty name of Jesus and His Lordship throughout the village. Strongholds came tumbling down. When we arrived back at campus and began to shout to the Lord, the Holy Spirit fell upon us and we danced and celebrated. God had given us the victory! The next Sunday several elders from the village came to church to investigate what was happening at this school! Numerous villagers began coming to the church and several became Christians; others were miraculously healed. After the march, we were greeted throughout the village with smiles and waves even by Muslims, who previously simply stared darkly at us!

It was around this time that the Moshi Bible School received a new name, Kilimanjaro Christian College and KCC was born! Each new building project became a new wineskin, and with the wineskins came new Holy Ghost wine and even a new thing.

Behold, I will do a new thing; now it shall spring forth; shall ye not know it? I will even make a way in the wilderness, and rivers in the desert. (Isa. 43:19 KJV)

There is a saying that more is caught than taught. Being planted into the hearts of the married students was the anointed vision of the power of husband/wife partnership ministry. Fresh revelation had opened their eyes! Their hearts were being prepared by the Holy Spirit for the fulfillment of the Spirit's promise made centuries before, *"In the last days,"* God *says, "I will pour out my Spirit on all people. Your sons and **daughters** will prophesy, your young men will see visions, your old men will dream dreams. Even on my servants, both men and **women**, I will pour out my Spirit in those days, and they will prophesy."* (Acts 2:17-18 NIV)

Quietly, without a word from us, the Holy Spirit was bringing forth a revolutionizing cultural shift. He was planting the seed in their minds. Strongholds of tradition were being silently demolished by the mighty hand of God—in His time! God was about to do something amazing. One more step was necessary before the cultural shift—pastors had to complete their education. Graduating the pastors would then financially free their wives to be able to study. And this was about to happen.

Graduation was the highlight of school life and certainly the students' lives. During the early morning hours, the church women would decorate with brilliant flower clusters from the frangipane trees and boughs of bougainvillea covered with blossoms of every shade of purple to rosy pinks, and graceful palm branches. The cooks would begin to prepare the fire in order to cook rice and beans enough to feed the whole crowd of about four hundred. Other women chased the scampering squawking chickens, who were trying to evade their intended destiny, fried chicken for the grads and their special guests. It was a grand occasion, a two-soda day. That was the determining factor. Two sodas meant it was truly a day of celebration! That was so very important to them, and we did our best to make it happen. Amazing, but fortunately for all of us who live there long-term, we actually acquired a taste for warm soda. It was more or less a necessity. We could be sure it was sterile if we uncapped the top ourselves! An uncapped bottle had the potential for another case of amoeba. It meant someone in the back may have helped themselves to a sip and then topped the bottle off with village water! The primary missionary life lesson was never drinking anything you didn't open yourself when you were away from your house.

Our very special friends, Richard and Pam Smoak could never do enough to bless us. Graciously they granted us the rental of their huge Gospel tent. It shaded hundreds of people from the intense equatorial sun. Churches rented *matatus* to bring their choirs to be a musical part of the grand celebration. All the men and women were decked out in paisley printed matching colorful outfits. Singing and swaying in synchronized rhythm they would really rock the place. Speeches were given, degrees conferred, and tassels were moved.

When a grad's name was called, the wife and family would SCREAM! The women would shout with the African *vigelele* (a loud noise made by saying la rapidly) and run to the front to shower the grad with gifts and decorate him or her with colorful tinsel garlands on their necks. The spouse would then give a hug or kiss. Tanzanians do not typically show affection in public, but on this day there was a special dispensation for a wife to kiss her man, something never done in public—a touch man to woman! In friendship men held hands with other men as they walked and women with women, but never with each other.

It was an explosion of joy with everyone clapping, shouting, and jumping. The Gospel choirs would sing and eventually everyone would join in and sing and dance in celebration of the goodness of God, who had done this great thing for them. Finally the graduates were invited to come forward for the anointing service. It was a sacred time of prayer as we placed our hands on them, anointed them with oil, and consecrated them for Holy Spirit empowered ministry of the Gospel. It was a profoundly moving moment to be chosen by God for the privilege of being a participant in such a holy act.

After pictures, hugs, and handshakes for all their special visitors, the grads were finally escorted to the feast. A special room was prepared for the graduates and one special guest. The tables were set with linens and spoons. The soon-to-be senior students dressed in black and white and waited on them in grand classy style. There was chicken, fresh cut fruit and veggies, potatoes, delicious fried African spinach, and the traditional rice and beans. It was a feast beyond belief and a Duncan Hines cake transported from America topped it off. It was so beautiful as I placed it on the table in the graduates' dining area. Only later did I notice the icing had melted by the heat of the day and slid off the cake. *Hamna shida* (No problem!) They didn't care. After all, Mama, that's what spoons are for. They were so gracious, so thankful. Graduation was the highlight of the school year, a blessed and glorious *two-soda day*!

Cultural Revolution: A Bible School for Women

In February of 2000, while preaching at our Maasai church at Ndinyika, the first announcement was made that a Bible school for women was to be launched in July 2000. It would be a one-week session exclusively for women between the regular school sessions. This school for women burned within my heart with a passion that only God could have placed there. To the extent that one afternoon as I prayed and labored over the school's inception, I found myself in agony of soul bearing down in a birthing position as a woman about to deliver a child. Out of those prayers was birthed something new and fresh for my beloved African sisters. Could this be the fulfillment of the prayer that I prayed in our Arusha garden in 1997? The day God told me I was praying for the women of Africa.

Our missionary business card motto was *"Reaching and Teaching for Jesus."* As His disciples sent to the nation of Tanzania, we knew Jesus had instructed us not only to reach the nation with the Gospel, but also to *"teach them to obey"* the things that He taught. Many church leaders in the region had not yet received training in the Word. Men and women were perishing without knowledge of the scriptures. In Psalm 103 we are exhorted to remember all God's benefits. How can one recall what he/she has never learned? The churches were filled with baby Christians lacking a solid foundation in the Word of God.

My people are destroyed for lack of knowledge. (Hosea 4:6 NKJV)

Our hearts' cry was to see that changed. Tanzanian women are the movers of society. They simply could not get away for the normal three-week session of the regular Bible school. According to the word God placed continually upon our hearts—discipleship—we moved forward as God had commanded. We did what was best for all—one week sessions for women between the regular Bible school terms. By the grace of God and the power of the Holy Spirit within me, I had committed to teach them God's Holy Word. The whole idea was radical—a Bible school for women! God's plan was revolutionary; in Jesus' mighty name cultural barriers were crashing down.

Two of the *women* in that tiny Maasai mud and stick church were among those to attend the first Tanzanian Women's Bible School in July. One a young teenage girl of about 15 received a copy of the Swahili Children's Picture Bible. After returning home ignited by the Spirit's fire, she approached her local Maasai elder for a stamped letter of approval to begin a children's Bible class. She began to teach the children and before long over one hundred ten village children were in attendance. During the next session of the Bible school, she boldly testified. Waving her official document high in the air, she spoke of God's tremendous blessing among the Maasai children. The women erupted in powerful praise to God— jumping, screaming, and dancing! Our prayer was to make Christ-like disciples that would make Christ-like disciples. God was indeed bringing the increase.

Weeks later, as we visited a church in Sanya Juu, the church women broke out in a grand celebration of joy and tears as the

Bible school for women was announced. In July, eight of those women came. One of them had serious issues with men and had developed a Jezebel spirit. She went home free from hatred and bitterness and every evil thing that oppressed her.

The following is a direct quote from the July 2000 newsletter:

*America, the women of Tanzania say ASANTE SANA (thank you very much). The miracle of the **Women's Bible College** owes its very life to all of you who have prayed and fasted for its birth over the last weeks. It was all we could have hoped for and more. **Sixty women** came down from the villages in the hills of Mount Kilimanjaro and Mount Meru and from the Maasai Steppe with their belongings on their heads for the week of a lifetime— beyond their wildest imagination. Even while writing this I (Marilyn) weep for joy and am in awe of the grace of God in the working of this glorious beginning. Apart from God, never could any of us have believed for such a thing! From bibi (grandmother) to kijana (teens) we began each day at 5 AM with prayers, 6 AM chores, 7:30-9:30 AM class, breakfast from 9:30-10:00, class until 1:00, lunch until 2:30 and then class again until 4:30 or 5:00. Dinner was followed by a preaching service in the evening. Each woman was given a new Bible with concordance and a Theology 1 course book. Because of the topic (Theology 1: Doctrine of God, Man, Angels, Satan), we discussed everything from praying prayers of faith to religious spirits to the Jezebel spirit (of which one was delivered), to homosexuality and pornography, to marriage and family. Many prayed to have soul ties broken from past sexual unions. Special emphasis was placed on reaching children while they are young. A cultural myth here is that children can't be saved until they are teens. The*

Holy Spirit gave me the most awesome example to use. He had me put the numbers 4, 5, 6 on the board to represent village children; reminding them that God used Balaam's donkey to get his attention, I asked, "Do you doubt the Holy Spirit's ability to witness to children's spirits about Jesus?" Then God had me put a 1 before each 4, 5, or 6 making them teens and saying, "In ten years without Christ they will all be sexually active, and then in ten more years they will all be dead of AIDS." Matthew 18:10 burned in their hearts, "Take heed that you do not despise one of these little ones, for I say to you that in heaven their angels always see the face of My Father who is in heaven." Over and over it was stressed God chose to bring them here to go to each of their home villages to teach all the women and children about Jesus' love for them. At closing we had such an intimate communion and foot washing service. Everyone was weeping, some hysterically. Something miraculous happened when their feet touched the water. The Spirit spoke to me, "This is the healing of a nation." Many later came forward and were baptized in the Holy Spirit. During the week some received physical healings, and everyone received something wonderful from Jesus. For the first time I saw joy on the face of a pastor's wife whom we wrote about previously whose two children were killed, poisoned by the Maasai, and whose last pregnancy ended this spring in a stillbirth.

One woman said, "In our village we have such poverty; we have nothing; we learn nothing. But here we have learned about the Holy Spirit and about Jesus. Now we are rich." THANK YOU! THANK YOU! THANK YOU—for every sacrifice and prayer you have made to make all of this possible.

Remembering the glory of it all still makes me weep! How God transformed their lives from shy, fearful, women to significant, courageous, empowered saints. The first term most had never owned a Bible or personally knew much of its contents. Many women had never been out of their villages. To them Langoni and Moshi must have seemed like the ends of the earth. Even now I realize surely they were in culture shock. They didn't even socialize much one with another the first part of the week. For a Tanzanian that was beyond unusual! In order to break the ice and any tribal barriers that may have existed, I demonstrated hugging with a few ladies. Then I set them free to do some hugging. They laughed and squeezed each other with unspeakable joy. It became one of their favorite *keep alert* activities as our days were both long and hot! There is no word in Swahili for the action of hugging so they all named it *huggi*. It was a western concept the ladies eagerly embraced. By the end of the week, everyone stood physically taller. Some had come with open sores on their legs. Just a week's worth of prayer and nourishing food had healed their bodies. God was doing a divine work inside and out!

My son (daughter), give attention to my words; Incline your ear to my sayings. Do not let them depart from your eyes; keep them in the midst of your heart; for they are life to those who find them, and health to all their flesh. (Proverbs 4:20-22 NKJV)

Education had empowered them; even their attitudes about themselves were changing. Self-esteem took a giant leap forward—now they were finding their acceptance in Jesus! *To the praise of the glory of his grace, wherein he hath made us accepted in the beloved.* (Eph. 1:6 KJV) Years of destructive baggage had been eliminated. Complete in God, they were able to gather in groups and engage in discussions about the days' lessons. They had become college students!

One Maasai woman slept the whole time. Certainly that must have been the only time in her life she ever sat down except maybe on a local mini bus, and that experience is anything but comfortable—more like a life or death adventure. But she passed her test. Troubled by this, I asked the Lord, "How could this be?" I felt He told me her spirit was awake. Those words were real encouragement for this worn out mama!

After the first term, a pastor came to visit to testify about his wife's transformation. She used to spend the day gossiping; now she only reads her Bible. He proclaimed how his love and admiration for her had grown. She was now an asset in the church! Every church that had women present in the Bible school for women was bursting with joy over the changes taking place in women's ministries at the local church. Other churched men who had fearfully forbidden their wives to participate in the ministry came to Terry and repented, begging for opportunities for their wives to come.

The main classroom difficulty for the women the first term was finding passages—getting everyone on the same verse was quite a task! A challenge to memorize the order of the books of the Bible by the second term was accepted, and they did it! From then on they were quick to find any reference.

All of this began with my two year fruit prayer, prayed while still living in Fredonia, NY and finalized by obedience to the fast God called me to in the first months in Tanzania. Certainly I didn't anticipate the greatness of His answer, but God knew! He was looking for a willing vessel to work through. I simply said, "Yes!"

During that time, I had attended a Western NY Aglow conference at Chautauqua Lake. When the seventy year old speaker asked, "Who will go?" In my heart I said, "I will go!" Simple prayers prayed by sincere saints can change a nation.

Ask of me, and I will make the nations your inheritance, the ends of the earth your possession. (Psalm 2:8 NIV)

On January 19, 2001 the sixty abundantly grateful women presented me with the following letter of thanks. I have copied it as beautifully and exactly as it was written directly from their hearts:

A WORD OF THANKS FROM THE BIBLE COLLEGE WOMEN

To God almight, our loving Father, be glory and honor forever! Amen!

To the Principal of the Bible College Baba Terry and Mama Merlyn our beloved, wonderful! Teacher, be our heartfelt gratitudes for the visions that you have for Tanzania! We want you to know that we are glad to have meet you and feed from what you offer from God! May God of love bless you abundantly.

We also have heartfelt gratitudes to our beloved sisters in Christ, Mama Shirley and Whitney and the women of America that gave their time, money Prayers and many other helps for the women of Tanzania. Please accept our heartfelt gratitudes for we have nothing to give worth of your love and care for us.

May God of love bless you!

We also take this opportunity to bless the children of America who gave their love to the children of Africa for sending the children's bible.

May God of Love bless you little lovely Children.

Lastly, we women of Tanzania are praying that God may give an ongoing heart of love, without forgetting our beloved sister, Cath and Tinah for being with us blessing us with worshiping.

Praying that we may all meet in heaven.

Again God bless you!

Please read Ef. 6:6-7

Here is the scripture she lovingly wanted us to read:

Not with eye service, as men pleasers; but as the servants of Christ, doing the will of God from the heart; with good will doing service, as to the LORD, and not to men. (Ephesians 6:6-7 KJV)

Perhaps one of the most profound impacts on a woman's life was the change in Mama Mbise. Years ago she and her husband, Elieta Mbise, left their family lands and went as missionaries to the Maasai. Formerly, the Maasai had been their enemies for good reason. Hadn't the Maasai gone on a rampage throughout their lands, robbing the grazing animals and molesting their women? Salvation brought such a change to the Mbise family that their hearts were filled with love and zeal for the lost among the Maasai. One day during the worship service of their newly planted church, an unknown Maasai poisoned and killed their little children as they played outside the church. It was a horrible tragedy of unknown proportions at that time. It was true that, years before, the Meru tribe had killed two mzungu Lutheran missionaries, but not a fellow Tanzanian missionary. It was an added burden when the couple's parents, who had opposed their move to the Maasai village, blamed their adult children for offending the ancestral family spirits. Some years later they had another son. I can still see the tormented face of sorrow and the fear of losing yet another son that drained her countenance as she sat in the women's Bible College. The great cloud of suffering that rested on her was lifted. God's grace sustains her; now she even smiles again. She is an example of the redeeming, healing power of the Spirit of Christ.

Jesus Christ is the same yesterday and today and forever. (Hebrews 13:8 NIV)

Gratitude to the Living God for the honor and privilege of loving these women of God, teaching them, knowing them, and calling them sisters fills my soul. None of us will ever be the same again.

Transitions

In 2001 after over five years of powerful Holy Spirit anointed ministry on countless bumpy roads, we made—actually my body made—the decision that enough was enough. According to my chiropractor, I had seven vertebrae and discs with problems. The pain was amazing, sometimes unbearable. Terry remained in Tanzania to close up the loose ends and to sell any accumulated household stuff not belonging to Mama Stella. I returned home alone for further chiropractic treatments only to find the practice now belonged to another Christian, Dr. Greg Dokka. After some treatments I felt a little better physically but remained lonely and emotionally drained. When the opportunity came to be with old friends in NY, quickly, I was on a plane. While I thought the trip was totally about visiting dear friends and receiving their encouragement, God had a greater plan. Behind the scenes the Holy Spirit was engineering life's circumstances to have His miraculous way in my life. Repeatedly Father God had a way of reminding me that, *"...My thoughts are not your thoughts, nor are your ways My ways," says the LORD. "For as the heavens are higher than the earth, so are My ways higher than your ways, and My thoughts than your thoughts.* (Isa 55:8-9 NKJV) My thoughts were focused on accepting that my days on the mission field were over. In the natural it was the case. But Jesus is supernatural!

Weary, I had given up and somehow I had forgotten my own healing message—that God is the God of the impossible. One of my favorites sayings when I preached was to tell people that Jesus is God *Almighty*—not God *some mighty*. Once again Almighty God was about to show Himself strong in my life. He had used my friend Maureen Fortner's invitation to visit her in western NY to put me in the vicinity of a miracle. After arriving I found out that an anointed healing evangelist was coming to Buffalo for a crusade. I called Maureen and excitedly told her, "I'll pay for the room if you will go with me." As a home-schooling mother of eight, it was a challenge and sacrifice for her, but off we went!

The worship was great; we were blessed by encountering the manifest presence of the Living God. During the service on the second day, the minister called out that someone had been cursed by witchcraft. When he broke the curse, there were three clicks in the atmosphere surrounding my back as the chains fell off. The power of darkness had been broken and my healing had begun. Before long I was mostly pain free. *"If you diligently heed the voice of the LORD your God and do what is right in His sight, give ear to His commandments and keep all His statutes, I will put none of the diseases on you which I have brought on the Egyptians. For I am the LORD who heals you."* (Ex 15:26 NKJV)

Simultaneously God was working on two continents! In Moshi Terry was busy at home finalizing things when the phone rang; it was a call from Mike Rothery. Seems God was about to use Mike again to rescue us and redirect our path. He had just received a call from an Australian friend, Rosemary Brice, inquiring if he knew anyone who might want to teach at the Bible school in Nairobi, Kenya. When Mike called and relayed the message to Terry, he excitedly responded, "Yes! Call her right back and tell her we'll do it." In America there was a miracle, and in Africa another one. *Trust in the LORD with all your heart, and lean not on your own understanding; in all your ways acknowledge Him, and He shall direct your paths.* (Pro 3:5-6 NKJV) And so I returned to Tanzania with a new freedom of movement and vigor for a fresh start in Kenya. God was still answering this often prayed prayer:

Even when I am old and gray, do not forsake me, O God, till I declare your power to the next generation, your might to all who are to come. (Ps 71:18 NIV)

Our final days in Tanzania were exciting as we celebrated our third graduation of the Bible school—the first as Kilimanjaro Christian College! Twenty students were graduated, and it was a grand *sherehe* (celebration). There were about four hundred in attendance and it was jubilant and colorful. Pastor Kiriama served as master of ceremonies and the valedictorian was Pastor Ndelelio Nanyaro. Both men were about to be launched as powerful ambassadors for Christ as future Bible school principals. In a dramatic moment, Terry before the huge crowd passed to Lazaro a beaded Maasai stick called *fimbo ya mamlaka,* meaning stick of authority! Everyone witnessed the passing of the baton! Lazaro Kiriama was now the principal of Kilimanjaro Christian College. Great applause, hooting and hollering erupted. After a powerful anointing service, we said our final farewells to the students, blessed them, and sent them out to do great exploits for God.

Two days later on a public mini bus we made our move—definitely reminiscent of the Beverly Hillbillies—only worse—to Kenya.

Our adventure as recorded in our *Tanzanian East African Tapestry:*

Off to Kenya: *After completion of this newsletter, we will pack up the computer and move over to the other side of Mount Kilimanjaro to Kenya, where our primary ministry will be at Nairobi Pentecostal Bible College. We are leaving tomorrow morning by bus with Terry's desk and chair, eight large containers, and six suitcases which will be tied to the roof of a mini bus! Immediately we will be settling into a Swahili language course in Limuru, a town about one hour drive west of Nairobi. We will try to greatly upgrade our Swahili language skills prior to settling into the new areas of ministry the Lord has opened for us in Kenya. The ministry at NPBC will basically be the same as in Moshi, teaching and ministering to pastors from East Africa. We will continue to minister in the local churches of our pastors and continue to hold conferences, seminars, evangelistic outreaches, etc. as the Lord continues to open doors. There is never any shortage of opportunities for ministry and we look forward to all that the Lord will do in the future in Kenya.*

It was time to say *"Jambo"* Kenya!

After completing my language study in Limuru, I was definitely charged to engage our Kikuyu gardener/guard in Swahili conversation only to discover the people around Nairobi for the most part spoke either Kikuyu or English, not Swahili. Unfortunately that was after I preached a whole sermon in a Nairobi Kikuyu church where no one had a clue what I was saying! I was frustrated and disappointed, but only temporarily! As usual, God was up to something! Fortunately we could freely speak English with most Kikuyu—at least we thought we could.

The Kikuyu tribe which predominately inhabited the region around Nairobi for some reason had a great difficulty with the letters "R" and "L." Whenever a word had an *"R"* they would substitute an *"L"* and vice versa. Terry Weaver became *Telly Weavel* and I was *Maliryn Weavel*. Lions were *rions* and so on. Our most embarrassing moments with the exchange were when visiting an English speaking Kikuyu church. Feeling the joy of the Lord, the Kikuyu pastor would loudly exclaim, "Let's *crap* for Jesus!" Words cannot express the startling effect that had on us! Traumatized inside by the shock and trying not to explode in hysterical laughter while maintaining composure on the outside was not an easy scenario. Fortunately, with everyone loudly clapping and joyfully celebrating, our muffled laughter was not too obvious. Needing to quickly adjust to Kikuyu Kenyan language culture became a high priority on our personal agenda.

Finding housing in Nairobi was very difficult because rents were very high compared to Tanzania. Frustrated by the situation, we were walking through the Sarit Centre Mall in Nairobi when we ran into the pastor's wife of Nairobi Lighthouse Church. Right there we asked for prayer, and the next day we found a wonderful house on the edge of a coffee plantation. It was a beautiful new house and we could rent it for $600 US a month. An enormous amount to be sure, but the best we could do. What we didn't know was that no one else had rented it because of the open location along the vast coffee plantation—making the property very vulnerable to thieves.

Due to this lack of security, the property had not been put on the approved list of rentals for foreign nationals and it had not been rented. We had no money and no furniture so we had no problem from thieves; they could look in our windows and see it wasn't worth it to even bother robbing us. That is except for our substitute guard who robbed us one Sunday morning while we were at church of almost every electrical thing we owned that was not locked up in Terry's office. Thank God our computers were in there! When we called the landlord to complain to him that we were really upset that the man he recommended had robbed us, General Hezron said, "Don't worry about him ever bothering you again. He's in prison—he emptied my internet café of its computers yesterday and won't be bothering anyone for some time."

Our house was grand, but the furnishings meager. For many months we had only four green plastic chairs which we used for sitting and dining and a mattress on the floor upstairs. We placed the chairs at the kitchen counter and basically sat at mouth level. One of our friends joked about our ability to just shovel that food right into our mouths. While in language school we ordered a bedroom set to be made so we would be comfortable at night. Later we added a dining table. Harry and Rosemary Brice, our coworkers at NPBC, told us of a woman who sold inexpensive handwoven wicker furniture. Soon the living room had a loveseat and two chairs. Now we had someplace to sit, but the grass made everyone's allergy prone nose run! A box of tissues was always nearby. From the beginning we had great fellowship with missionaries like Phil and Starlene Harmon, the Brices, our Elim reps Ken and Ibby

VanDruff, our safari friends, John and Anne Martin, and Kenyan friends John and Jackie Mesesi Magangi

Celebrating American holidays overseas was an important way we missionaries stayed in touch with our own culture. One year for the Fourth of July, we traveled from Nairobi to Nakuru to visit our dear Assembly of God Kenyan missionary friends, John and Anne Martin. Our celebration plans included viewing game at Lake Nakuru National Park and having an old fashioned holiday picnic. I told them I had a really special surprise for our picnic lunch. In a Nairobi supermarket close to the American Embassy, we had found Doritos! It was an American *treasure* that had been shipped via container to Mombasa and then trucked to Nairobi. You can imagine the exorbitant inflated price on such an item. But it was the Fourth! We were excited as we purchased the prized item and secretly transported it to the Martins for our special surprise. But we were the ones to be surprised!

During our safari in the park we came upon a picnic table on a beautiful lush green hillside. We had had a peaceful day and to this point had not encountered any cats—therefore we were all a little disappointed. No matter, our special surprise was about to be revealed. By this time the Martins were a bit intrigued to discover what all the secrecy was about. After parking the vehicle, making sure to leave all doors ajar—just in case a cat also famished should show up—we unloaded the picnic, placed everything on the table and all gathered together to share the still unknown contents of the basket. As I triumphantly revealed the long anticipated prize, a bag of American Doritos chips, da daaaaa the Martins gave a shout of joy.

Simultaneously from bushes nearby, there was a wild boisterous battle cry! A huge male baboon charged at us. Gasping, we all jumped backwards in terror. In that split second, the baboon jumped onto the table, grabbed the chips, and sped away to the center of a field about a hundred yards within our view. We were shocked! Gone! Our delicious Doritos were gone before we could act. In our frustration and sorrow we all watched as, now settled in, he sat up straight, carefully opened our bag of Doritos with his teeth, and began to eat them. It was as if he were taunting us. Proudly he would draw one out, give a flick of the wrist, then proceed to put a chip into his mouth. Chip by chip he devoured our Doritos; we were furious!

A few minutes later the Doritos were forgotten when a park guide directed us to a tree where four lions had trapped a leopard. It was an amazing stand-off. Somehow all five of the beasts were entangled in the same tree—and it wasn't all that big. Eventually, the leopard got away, but not before some very loud growly Fourth of July *fireworks* in a nearby bush!

Safaris were always fun and amazing times. We assumed our Kenyan friends as citizens of one of the finest game countries in the world would have experienced a safari adventure. We were astonished to discover how many of our students at Nairobi Pentecostal Bible College had never even seen a giraffe. One of our weekly responsibilities while teaching at NPBC was to shepherd a cell group consisting of our students. Each year the group planned a special year-end event. We decided to do something different for them and rented the park's bus for a spectacular adventure to the Nairobi National Park. Not far from city-center is located a true safari park with a great variety of wildlife including lion, cheetah, and leopard, rhinos, and hippos. As we entered the park and came around the bend, the students were thrilled to discover several long-legged giraffes gracefully crossing the road directly in front of us. But the best was yet to come! One of the special events planned for the day was our picnic. There were about twenty of us plus Larry and Joyce Lambert, a British couple, who also worked at the school. When lunchtime arrived, the driver parked the bus at the picnic area. Most of the students crowded into the first open cement shelter. After everyone was served, the rest of us *relaxed* in a second shelter. We prayed together; everyone shouted, "Amen," and started to eat. Once again we heard a loud obnoxious battle cry and several baboons attacked our table. *Do they have it in for Wazungu?* Larry had his sandwich taken out of his mouth as he bit into it. The baboons grabbed everything they could as we froze—too startled to move. Our students were hysterical with laughter! Fortunately, that day we had lots of extras; we had learned that lesson on the Fourth of July!

Daily exercise, whether occasionally on safari or walking in the coffee plantation after class, was essential. Everything seemed to require so much more energy to stay on top of than in America. Again banking was an issue; once our money was frozen in the banks for several weeks. The solution was to cash checks at an Indian exchange at the Sarit Center—only to find out they photo copied our check for $1000 and submitted it twice to our American bank. Walking in the deserted coffee plantation behind our house reduced our cultural stress and refreshed us as we watched the playful antics of our two dogs—Scruffy (an adoptee from NPBC) who was the typical yellow coated African variety and Tiny (inherited from former Nairobi Baptist missionaries) who was a rambunctious Jack Russell with a lot of attitude. Both loved chasing through the plantation after rabbits or other small rodents. One day Scruffy charged the swamp in the lowlands and sent a large group of majestic crowned cranes squawking and flying rapidly away. Animal Planet would have loved it! For Scruffy everything was a game. They were a great deal of fun and protection for us.

Tiny took her guarding seriously! She hated strangers—which was anyone who entered her territory, whether friend or foe. Each night whenever our night guard came to work, she would charge out the back door toward the guard shack barking ferociously at him and then bite his ankles. Even on his nights off she would perform the same drill minus the biting part. Out the door she would run to the empty guard house where the guard normally stationed himself and bark furiously at nobody. But God had sent Tiny to us for a purpose—not only companionship, but for protection. If ever there was a type A personality dog, it was Tiny. She was constantly on alert. Even if it was a mosquito on the bedroom wall, she would put her nose on the wall directly under it and stand there at attention warning us of its presence until we dealt with it.

Any little noise and she would be barking. In the evening if anyone walked by the compound, she immediately barked ferociously setting up a chain of events. Tiny's barking alerted Scruffy; Scruffy's barking woke up the sleeping guard. The guard would then either loudly blow his whistle or discharge a warning arrow whenever thieves were in the neighborhood.

One day while we were walking along the footpath in the coffee plantation, Tiny definitely earned her biscuits. Scruffy was scurrying about thoroughly sniffing the area; Terry was walking behind him along the narrow footpath, relaxed and enjoying the cool afternoon air. Suddenly Terry noticed a black snake slithering onto the path. Quickly he stopped, turned around, and called out to me, "There's a snake on the path ahead!" "What should I do?" I asked. He told me to go up the mound. Someone had bulldozed a deep crater-like pond to refresh the local cattle that grazed in the area and left a huge mound of dirt on the side of the path toward us. Moving swiftly along I climbed the steep crater's edge. Just as I was feeling safe, the snake, now totally annoyed by the dogs and us, decided to raise its body and spread its black hood. To this Terry then yelled, "It's a cobra— RUN!" Kicking up the dirt with my heels, I took off. All the while I had been calling to the dogs. I was terrified they would be bitten and suffer a painful death! We had seen enough dogs die. Finally arriving safely at the top of the next ridge, I noticed our Tiny still on the path charging the snake—rapidly darting in and out, over and over! Again and again I called, begging her to come. Finally, as if she now knew we were safe, she suddenly backed off and charged up after us. It wasn't until one day telling this story that I realized how God used her to protect us. Later, as we thought about the event, we realized that we had encountered the snake in the exact area we used to call Rat Road. Almost every day we saw furry gray mouse-like critters scurrying about in the area. But recently we had seen none and had even remarked wondering where they had gone. Hmmm? Another mystery solved!

We enjoyed the big city life for a while. It was so revitalizing to be teaching and worshipping in English. We had the unique privilege of teaching students from many other African countries including Sudan, Burundi, Rwanda, Congo, Uganda, and Eritrea. Our hearts were particularly stirred by the tragic testimonies of our male students from Rwanda and Sudan. We prayed about going to Rwanda to plant a Bible school, but God closed the door. He had more plans for us in Tanzania.

Pastor Nanyaro, our former KCC student, contacted us in Nairobi and invited us to come teach at his newly formed Bible school in Manyara. He knew the condition of my back precluded ministry in his area. So his letter informed us that while we were living in Kenya and actively engaged in ministry there, the Japanese government was restoring the Tanzanian road system, including surfacing the road to the Ngorongoro Crater. It was destiny—God had literally *paved* the way for our return! A trip was planned for us to visit and teach there while we were on holiday from NPBC. We were now driving a town car and were amazed that as we turned off the main road from Arusha and headed toward Manyara there was the most beautiful road. It even had lines painted on it. Mto wa Mbu was transformed. The beautifully paved main street was lined with banana trees, especially of the meaty red-skinned variety. Nestled comfortably beneath the shade of the broad leaves were the local merchants desperately attempting to engage any even slightly interested tourist in barter. Interest meant merely looking in their direction! There were two basic groups. First were the brightly adorned and constantly chatting *mamas* (women) selling locally grown fruits and vegetables. These were conveniently piled in sets of three or five items called a *funga*, usually spread out on an old kanga lying on the ground or placed in groups upon the top of a huge upside down yellow bucket. Seated close by were the artisans, who proudly displayed every variety of delicately carved game animal. Elephants, lions, hippos, gazelles, and giraffes stood proudly by, towering over the large selection of salad spoons and small instruments made of a small rectangular piece of wood with very thin metal strips attached to be plucked by strong, rhythmic fingers. All were placed on a makeshift portable wooden box or dirty grubby cloth left over from a formerly purchased bag of maize. Both businesses were totally portable. At the end of the day the vendors simply picked up their wares placed any remaining produce inside their display material and proceeded home.

The trip from Mto wa Mbu up the switchback road to the top of the escarpment was now only ten minutes instead of hours. Amazing! We were rejoicing at the way the Lord had answered our prayers for the roads to be paved. While visiting Nanyaro to encourage him and teach at his new school, our hearts were set on fire with renewed vision. Later in the week, Pastor Nanyaro asked us to partner together with him in this outreach to the men and women from Mto wa Mbu to the Ngorongoro Crater.

We returned to Kenya. It was decision time! Certainly we did not want to deviate from God's perfect will. One afternoon I sat in my upstairs office overlooking the thousands of scrubby green coffee trees lining the Kenyan hillside in rows like miniature soldiers. What to do? I had called out to God to direct us yet once again. During the prayer time, the Holy Spirit impressed upon my heart to listen to our Elim ordination tape. On it were these words prophesied by our Elim sister, Nancy Clark, *"You will be as countrymen."* There was only one place that fit that description—Tanzania was calling us home.

After a brief trip to America to confirm with Elim and our supporters that this was indeed the will of God, we contacted a moving company, gave Scruffy to the Harmons, and returned to Tanzania.

Behold, I will do a new thing, now it shall spring forth. Shall you not know it? I will even make a road in the wilderness, and rivers in the desert. ...Because I give waters in the wilderness and rivers in the desert, to give drink to My people, My chosen, this people I have formed for Myself; they shall declare My praise. (Isa 43:19-21 NKJV)

Returning to Moshi was wonderful for many reasons. Helping to establish a new Bible School was the main reason for our return, but we were overjoyed at the prospect of having an opportunity to get to know Brian's new wife, Janine.

Seems that at the same time God was moving us to Nairobi God was beginning to dramatically change Brian's life. Each year Brian furloughed during his organization's missions conference. As a typical middle-aged woman with grand-children on her mind, each year I would inquire after his trip home, *"Meet anyone special?"* Finally the year we moved to Kenya he said he had seen someone, but that she felt she was called to China. The next year he again saw the beautiful Janine Cava. This time during their conversation she happened to mention she was open to whatever the Lord had for her. It was missions, but no longer necessarily China. Later, a friend invited Janine to accompany some others who were planning a trip to Tanzania in the fall. Missions trips are busy times, so although they were together, it wasn't until right before time to depart for the airport that they had some moments to chat alone. Later at the airport Brian said to himself, "If she turns around and looks at me when she leaves, then I will know to pursue the relationship." She turned and looked right at him. He wrote to us later that day and said that he thought there were *"sparks when he looked into her eyes."* During prayer the Lord gave us this word for Brian that he needed "to come home and cement this thing." Two weeks later he was on a plane for America. Then on December 23, 2002 together with our son, Eric and his wife, Liz, Terry and I met Brian and Janine at the JFK Airport in New York City. We all loved her immediately. Our family was now complete. Brian returned to Tanzania on Christmas Day and Janine to Alabama. They were engaged by phone in February and married in April. In June 2003, Reverends Brian and Janine Weaver moved into the Moshi, Tanzania house we vacated when we moved to Nairobi.

Manyara Moments: Fulfilled Prophesy

Relationships are the building blocks of ministry in East Africa. In His divine providence in 1998, the Holy Spirit led us to minister in the Manyara-Karatu region located west of Arusha and Moshi toward the Serengeti. Our relationship began by taking the *Jesus Film* to the Manyara and Karatu areas and beginning to minister in the local churches. These outreaches had begun to break up the fallow ground and given us inroads with the Iraqw tribe, the largest people group inhabiting the Karatu-Manyara region. Famine relief and the women's conferences had convinced the Iraqw of Christ's love to them through us.

Located along the edge of the escarpment a short distance from Manyara are two large safari lodges where tourists stay while travelling to the Serengeti or visiting the amazing regional wildlife parks. After dropping off the tourists entrusted to their care, the safari truck drivers would go carousing in the town of Manyara a place with many bars and many more prostitutes. Spiritual darkness had taken a foothold; but into that darkness a new Bible school was being born.

AIDS had killed nearly every driver in one of the Arusha-based safari companies. The long term effects had devastated the economy of Manyara. Now AIDS orphans challenged the resources of Manyara's extended family members trying to raise them. After three seasons of drought, a great famine had hit the area—the people were skin and bone—some from disease; others from starvation. We were stunned when we visited Pastor Nanyaro's church to preach and saw the formerly robust congregation with their bones showing and clothes literally hanging off their bodies. They were destitute for food. Everyone was hungry! Two thousand pounds of maize were immediately distributed in the community, but it was only enough for one month. We sent out a cry to America for help and our mission partner's response was overwhelming. By the end of the drought, we were thankfully able to distribute over ten tons of life sustaining maize.

For many reasons the women of Manyara suffer greatly. Women had many mouths to feed—their own children and the orphans thrust upon them by family members who had succumbed to AIDS. There were no real opportunities for financial gain. Al Barrett of Threads of Hope had given two sewing machines, and we sent two women for training to Nairobi, Kenya hoping to develop a sewing program. It wasn't enough to overtake the severity of the poverty. With so few jobs available, many women continued to resort to prostitution. The situation was a tragic cycle of death that needed to be broken! The only lasting solution to the problem could be found in Jesus.

Following the leading of the Holy Spirit, we scheduled our first women's conference in Manyara. There is a Swahili proverb, *"If you educate a woman you are educating society."* For three days the Holy Spirit empowered our meetings. The local government building was packed to capacity with over five hundred ladies inside and fifty more outside with heads tilted attentively, listening at every door and window. Pagans, prostitutes, Muslims, and religious women attended and over fifty of them surrendered their lives to Jesus as Savior.

Together with Carol Ballsmith, a worship leader, and Gail Arbeiter, a nurse— both from the Buffalo, New York area—we began by teaching on the heart of God and His desire for His daughters to passionately love Him. Using teachings on the tabernacle intertwined with anointed Swahili worship, Carol led the women into a deeper understanding of God's passionate desire for women to worship Him. Desperately in need of an encounter with God, they cried out and He heard their cry. For the first time, these ladies corporately experienced the manifest presence of God.

Having arrived spiritually impoverished, the ladies were being blessed beyond measure. Another blessing—the *men* of Pastor Nanyaro's church came with him and cooked lunch for the women for all three days! Everyone was amazed at this! Men sweating outside doing women's work so women could relax inside at the feet of Jesus! Absurd! That spoke volumes to the crowd and stirred up a few village demons.

Truth sets captives free. Understanding sexuality and the women's monthly menstrual cycle was new revelation to them. God used Gail to teach these precious uneducated, women about the birds and the bees and STDs. They had no knowledge of where babies came from. After all, nine months are a long time. Together Gail and I taught the Swahili AIDS course written by Kenyan missionary, Sharon Higgins. Horrified faces listened as knowledge was presented that AIDS could also be spread by using an infected person's toothbrush. More terrifying was the *aha* moment when they grasped the understanding of the possibility of AIDS transmission during the common practice of using the same razor blade on many initiates during the rite of circumcision or traditional local tribal cuttings—without using a fresh blade on each person or disinfecting the used one with *Jik*. Most had never heard of this bleach product, let alone the process of disinfecting something.

Powerfully God was moving! Not wanting to leave the men spiritually behind, the ladies had been encouraged to invite the village men to the afternoon crusade on the third day. Brian and his new wife Janine had been invited to preach the closing meetings. When a village elder called a political meeting during the powerful crusade, the devil tried to strike a blow to divert male attendance. One quite elderly man resisted the call to go; weeping, he gave his life to Jesus. I felt so strongly—if for no other reason, we were there *for such a time as this* for him!

In the final closing moments of our meeting the Village Chairman, a man in a position of great honor and authority, unexpectantly appeared. We were officially invited back by him to use the local government building anytime we wanted. He presented us with a letter stating the village was so grateful for our having chosen the area for our future Bible school, (at that time we were meeting in a local bar unused in daylight hours) and for the recent teachings—particularly those on AIDS, health, and family education. He wrote concerning AIDS, "... many are died and rest are suffering from that disease which has no prevention or cure." During the conference, God made it clear that His holy plan was to sanctify them—spirit, soul, and body. *Now may the God of peace Himself sanctify you completely; and may your whole spirit, soul, and body be preserved blameless at the coming of our LORD Jesus Christ. He who calls you is faithful, who also will do it.* (1 Thess. 5:23-24

NKJV) God's way was the only way of sure protection: one man and one woman for a lifetime.

God did a great work among the area women in Manyara. And He was not finished! We moved to the Karatu District about another thirty minutes from Manyara on the paved road proceeding toward the Ngorongoro Crater. Along the main road were brightly stained orange-red buildings. Because of continual drought conditions and very little grass to hold the rusty earth, the area's orange dirt has permeated the stucco of every building, coating them with layer upon layer of orange-colored dust. Expensive safari vehicles with wealthy clients pass through daily on their way to the Ngorongoro Crater or the Serengeti National Park. The travelers are in great contrast to the austerity of this town with orange-colored buildings.

In the village of Karatu, the Lutherans had a clean guest house with *mzungu* food, and often we or our visitors would stay there. From there we would proceed daily to the small off-road village. It was certainly one of the most unusual conferences with a great battle in the heavenlies over the souls of precious village women. Our host church was the church of Pastor James Sirikwa and his wife, Dorcas. She was a vibrant Christian with tremendous zeal for the Lord. One term while her husband had been away at KCC, Dorcas had been violated. Following healing prayer, she was emotionally restored and became a powerful example of God's grace to renew a life. She had chosen not to remain a victim to her attacker, but to move forward in forgiveness and, therefore, freedom. Her passion for God made her an excellent candidate for the Bible School for Women and later as a student at KCC. Her excellent leadership and organizational skills together with her godly attitude set her apart. So when visitors were coming, to hold a women's conference in Karatu, I called on Dorcas to organize it.

Upon arrival in the village, we all noticed the sisters had worked hard to transform the courtyard of the village into a shaded pavilion. Skillfully they had sewn together remnants of maize bags to shade the audience from the hot African sun. It covered a large span of at least 50 x 50 feet. Under it were rows and rows of simple backless benches carried from homes and churches by brightly dressed ladies—balancing them on their heads!

By the second day, the center section of our creative tarp was sagging terribly, making worship difficult. These women loved to move in human chains dancing before the Lord and the "ceiling" was slapping them in the face. To solve the problem, one of the industrious deacons took a sturdy log about six inches in diameter and carefully positioned it in the middle of the make-shift tarp. He secured it to the best of his ability. Sometime later, that log tragically fell onto an impoverished older woman. She collapsed injured to the ground. We gathered around her to pray and up she jumped. She took her seat again and spent the rest of the day celebrating with us. Not even a headache!

Shortly after that episode, other things started to change. It was as if were we trudging through miry clay. We were pressing in, but we seemed to be getting nowhere in the Spirit. It was then that the Lord had my eyes fall on a strange woman in our midst. Although she was dressed like the others, her face had a greenish appearance with dark sunken hollowed eyes—almost skeletal in appearance. As soon as I noticed her, I turned to Mary Navarro, our anointed worship leader. Precisely, at the same moment, our spiritual eyes were opened. We mouthed to each other—"She is a witch." Approaching Dorcas, I then inquired, "Who *is* that woman?" She was a member of a nearby church. In His grace, God had opened our eyes to see the cause of the confusion—an enemy in disguise. We, Gospel warriors, were battling the forces of darkness again that day as we prayed for her deliverance. *For we wrestle not against flesh and blood, but against principalities, against powers, against the rulers of the darkness of this world, against spiritual wickedness in high places.* (Eph. 6:12 KJV)

While we were battling demons in Karatu, Terry and Nanyaro were about to head out to the bush for a journey of epic proportions. They were headed to the Yaeda Valley—a place where the devil had a foothold but where the Light of God was about to penetrate.

And you, being dead in your trespasses and the uncircumcision of your flesh, He has made alive together with Him, having forgiven you all trespasses, having wiped out the handwriting of requirements that was against us, which was contrary to us. And He has taken it out of the way, having nailed it to the cross. Having disarmed principalities and powers, He made a public spectacle of them, triumphing over them in it. (Col. 2:13-15 NKJV)

Many years before that destiny-filled day, I stood praying in Nanyaro's church by an open window. Transfixed by the vastness of the land before me, I paused for a moment. As I continued to gaze out the window, the Holy Spirit spoke to me, "Pray that I might send forth laborers, for the white is on the harvest and the harvest is ripe." I was facing in the direction of the Yaeda Valley, the valley of the Barbaiq and Hadzabe. Passionately I prayed that prayer. Little did I realize that those laborers would be my husband and the pastor of the church where I now prayed.

On two continents God's saints had been called to pray to break up the fallow ground and prepare the way. The year of the first encounter with the Barbaiq and Hadzabe, Global Family Fellowship had a missions dinner targeting Tanzania. On the tables for each guest was placed the names of the unreached peoples groups of Tanzania for the member's prayer focus that year. Together with the saints of GFF, the prayers of God's people all along the East Coast of the USA plowed that soil with their faith-filled prayers. Those prayers put all the right people in the right place at the right time as God was about to orchestrate His plan.

When we moved the women's conference to Karatu, Pastor Nanyaro and Terry loaded the Land Rover with supplies: water, a tent, sleeping bags, food, extra fuel, and extra tires, then headed in the direction of the Yaeda Valley. Our 2004 November/December issue of our newsletter, *Weaver's East African Tapestry,* recorded Terry and Nanyaro's amazing safari into the dangers of the unknown African bush. In Terry's own words:

*We knew the **Hadzabe bushmen** live around Lake Eyasi (40 x 5 mile soda lake south of the Serengeti), but since there are no good roads and no real towns, we had no idea how to make contact. There was one dirt track to Lake Eyasi from the main road, so after asking the Lord for guidance, we headed off into the bush. After nearly three hours of driving, passing no vehicles or towns and few people, we reached Lake Eyasi and decided to eat some lunch under a tree. While eating, we noticed we were being watched from the bush by a man. I offered him a banana, and discovered he was Hadzabe and could speak some Swahili. After cutting him half our bunch of bananas for his family, he invited us to visit his family. So we walked back into the bush and met **our first Hadzabe family group living in "nests" under trees.*** We learned that they *worship spirits. Each month when there is no moon, the spirits visit them and tell them when and where to hunt. After a successful hunt they sacrifice the animal's organs to the spirits. They had heard of people who worship someone called Yesu. We agreed to return and tell them all about him! Returning, we gave a lift to young man walking alone through the bush who just happened to be **Barbaiq.** His uncle just happened to be an elder in the village and just happened to be an old friend of Nanyaro's. He gave us directions to his village over the other side of the mountain.*

We told him to tell his uncle that in one month his old friend Nanyaro and an mzungu would come to see him. And they had some "Good News" for him.

That was the beginning. Next was the decision to build a new Bible school with the divine purpose of training laborers to target the surrounding unreached areas. God had already spoken it to us; it had come as a word of prophecy. Years before after a great ministry time in the region, as we were about to begin our descent from Manyara to Mto wa Mbu, looking in the direction of the present school, out of my mouth came the words, "We *should build a Bible school there.*"

Recent events indicated that the season had arrived. God had planted a seed and it was time for the seed to germinate. Training indigenous pastors to minister to their own people, in their own language, was our missions strategy for enduring ministry. To do this we needed to be accessible to the Yaeda Valley. We searched together with Nanyaro for property. After a few setbacks, we decided upon a property located along the terracotta escarpment overlooking the lake. Lake Manyara Christian College is situated between the tiny Manyara Airport (actually a landing strip) and the luxurious Lake Manyara Serena Safari Lodge. Because of its fantastic location, we had glorious views of the area including the lake. And our road was maintained by the safari lodge!

From the school it was about a kilometer to the main road—near enough for the day students to use public bus transportation. This glorious piece of property was purchased by money given by our dear friends at Global Family Fellowship, Dunedin, Florida during their annual missions conference. Their global perspective helped Tanzania change God's world.

In 2005, a team of men led by Pastor Chris Lonneville from the Full Gospel Community Church of Warsaw, New York came and built the fifty by thirty foot open structure to be used primarily as a lecture hall and seminar building. The fired clay brick structure was built in only ten days. The Tanzanians working along the *Wazungu* (white men of European descent) nicknamed the American builders *tembos*, Swahili for elephant. The Africans were amazed at their size, relative to the typical Tanzanian, and especially the speed in which they worked. Before long the classroom building they constructed would have an integral role in advancing the Kingdom of God to unreached people groups.

Behind the beautiful brick classroom building, a traditional mud, stick, and grass kitchen was built. Daily portions of *chai* loaded with milk and sugar, rice and beans, or *ugali* (corn meal) and *supu* (vegetable soup) were necessary to keep the class energized. The only problem was keeping them awake after the sugar overload from the tea or the delicious lunch.

At the rear of the property, separate brick toilet and bath facilities facing in opposite directions were built for the men and the women. Everyone was thrilled, especially me! Before our *choo* had been a shallow hole in the ground; its walls were constructed of rickety sticks with grass woven throughout the openings. I was grateful for the privacy. Basically the men just headed out in every direction and we ladies would form a line!

By 2006 with the help of another building team led by John Wicks from Faith Chapel, Syracuse, New York, the campus was completed. Those guys built the sister building to the original classroom building. In ten days they built a fifty–two by thirty foot building. Again the Africans just couldn't believe the skill and speed with which they completed the project. The new building became a multi-purpose structure, housing a library, guest teacher quarters, men and women's dormitory, and offices. Before the building was built, the Hadzabe and Barbaiq students coming in from the bush were sleeping on the floor of the classroom building. Even then they were thrilled. They had never slept on a mattress before in their lives. They were so grateful to wake up without aching joints from the cold and/or dampness. With the new structure we were able to provide them with beds for those mattresses, and a little privacy. The students were so excited about the library, which further advanced the college into becoming a learning center for the glory of God.

Our quarters were a cement block room with a closed-in ceiling made of plywood. This would keep any furry critters that ran on the rafters during the night from dropping in for an uninvited visit. At the end, the room was divided into two U-shaped spaces. In one, Terry had installed a western toilet which we flushed by pouring water into the tank. It was wonderful! No need to traipse outside in the middle of the night to the *choo*. Outside attached to the roof was an elevated black tank which a hired man daily filled with water. After absorbing the sun all day, by afternoon it provided a quick— very quick—refreshing warm wonderful shower.

I was so grateful for the indoor bathroom. No more trauma during middle of the night potty breaks! Just over the hill at the base of the escarpment was the Lake Manyara National Park. The year before, a marauding leopard had taken up residence in the dining hall of a nearby compound. Tanzanian game parks have no fences and predators will wander wherever they smell food. Leopards are stealthy hunters and not easily detected as they move about in the bush. Hungry leopards have been known to be drawn by the odor of meat and then linger to attack unsuspecting humans.

We loved being able to stay on site. Occasionally after classes finished at Lake Manyara Christian College, Terry and I would leave the LMCC compound and walk along the dirt road to the nearby hotel located on the edge of the escarpment. We walked out of third world into absolute luxury! For a few moments we would relax with a cup of tea. Directly below us was the Lake Manyara Game Park. Having taken our binoculars, we could gaze upon the wildlife grazing in the plains below while sipping our *chai*. Counting giraffe or elephant was usually easy. And although undetectable even through binoculars, we always knew the location of the lions from the large number of parked safari vehicles! For a few moments the destitute situation of the Iraqw people would escape us. Upon leaving, however, reality would quickly return as there lounging along the edges of the pool were the desperate prostitutes of Manyara waiting for foreign customers. Sin has a consequence; one day those selfish unsuspecting tourists would realize they had taken something more than photos home from Tanzania.

Walking back and forth along the dusty road connecting the school with the safari lodge, we became friends with the many *duka* merchants selling creatively carved African tourist treasures. We had opportunities to encourage the Christians among them and one of them asked us for a Bible. I told him yes, with the condition that he would start a Bible study there for all the souvenir merchants. He agreed and we gave him one.

Later several others who had joined the study asked for one. What a joy to behold the group not only were they continuing to meet, but growing. God was at work!

Our Lake Manyara Christian College compound was becoming an asset to the whole community. Standing tall on the escarpment overlooking Lake Manyara, those two beautiful buildings became a symbol of a *New Presence* in Manyara.

Even as God was making new inroads in the lives of the people of Manyara, He was still at work in Moshi redeeming those bound in paganism and false religion. Returning home to Moshi I was honored to have an opportunity to speak at a conference Janine, our daughter-in-law, was hosting. It was an all-area Moshi women's meeting and she had rented a large hall on the Hindu compound for the event. Each time God grew me through the challenges and also opened up greater understanding of the people to whom He had called us to minister. I felt directed by the Spirit of God to share an encouraging message focused on God's thoughts about his daughters found in a little book I had written, *Fervent Love, God's Passionate Heart for His Daughters.* At the end of the message, a powerful anointing for evangelism came upon me. I knew that I was to give a Gospel invitation to receive Jesus as Savior. The plan of salvation was given, and absolutely no one moved. I was stunned; the anointing pressing inside me confirmed I was to do this. For a minute I paused—what to do? The Holy Spirit quickened me. I turned to the translator and said, "Do not translate this!" Powerfully emboldened by the Holy Spirit, in English, I began to take authority in the mighty name of Jesus! Loudly—very loudly—I was mad now at the devil's plan to hinder the work of the Lord—I began to bind every spirit of distraction. I bound every interfering religious spirit; next I prayed according to 2 Corinthians 4:4 and asked God to remove any spiritual blindness from their minds. Then in the name of Jesus, I loosed courage and salvation into that hall. I turned back to my translator and said, "Now you can translate." To the ladies I said, *"If you want to receive Jesus as your Savior, come out of your seats NOW!"* Quickly rising out of their seats, they moved forward with a fresh purpose. Over forty beautiful women came—some running—down the aisles to invite Jesus into their lives. No one was more amazed than me! Jesus said to do it—I did it! And glory to God it worked! I witnessed God set many women free because not because I am special but because I made a choice to choose to operate in the authority Jesus had given me. Although on previous occasions I had exercised authority, I had never done it quite so loudly and so publically. Privately or publically, Jesus is faithful to perform His Word. *"Assuredly, I say to you, whatever you bind on earth will be bound in heaven, and whatever you loose on earth will be loosed in heaven."* (Matthew 18:18 NKJV)

That wonderful day—truly salvation was loosed in that place.

A Mission within a Mission:

The Story of the Barbaiq

Our vision for targeting unreached people groups in Tanzania had been inspired in many ways. First, the Holy Spirit began stirring Terry's heart with the desire to reach out to the unreached peoples of Tanzania. Shortly thereafter, he had heard about an "East African Unreached Peoples Conference" being held in Nairobi, Kenya. We sponsored Lazaro to attend the conference and bring back information concerning the unreached tribes. Upon his return, he reported on six unreached people groups in Tanzania: the Wazaramo, the Wakwere, the Wamang'ati or Barbaiq, the Waudzungwa, the Wahadzabe, and sections of the Wamaasai. Renewed passion for reaching the lost was ignited within Terry and Lazaro as they strategized together. Now their goal was to impart the same passionate vision to the Bible school students—that as fully functional members of the Body of Christ they, too, were responsible for reaching lost souls! Jesus had included these Tanzanian disciples in the Great Commission when He said: *"Go into all the world and preach the gospel to every creature. He who believes and is baptized will be saved; but he who does not believe will be condemned. And these signs will follow those who believe: In My name they will cast out demons; they will speak with new tongues; they will take up serpents; and if they drink anything deadly, it will by no means hurt them; they will lay hands on the sick, and they will recover."* (Mark 16:15-18 NKJV) They had been equipped by the Word. Now it was time for the students of Kilimanjaro Christian College to move beyond their territory and become Gospel missionaries. God was about to give them new marching orders. Souls were at stake.

Our next term at the Bible school included a course on prayer and missions. The way was prepared for the Holy Spirit to do His work and align us all with the will of God for Tanzania. Taught by Rev. Andy Zack from Love Joy Gospel Church in Buffalo, New York, the course challenged the pastors to accept the biblical mandate to take the Gospel as Jesus directed, *"...and you will be my witnesses in Jerusalem, and in all Judea and Samaria, and to the ends of the earth."* (Acts 1:8) The students' hearts responded to the Macedonian call to accept their responsibility as full members of the body of Christ and to take the Gospel out to unreached peoples.

Up to this point in time, the mindset of most Tanzanians was that missionary work was the responsibility of *Wazungu*. While the church in Tanzania understood the need for local evangelism, they did little missions work beyond their own villages. After the completion of the missions course, powerful discussions ensued. Finally Terry challenged the students to devise a workable plan to reach out to those unreached people groups. By the end of the term, a plan had been formulated. The pastors had formed three coalitions of churches and targeted three of the unreached people groups in Tanzania. They were determined to raise up a missionary from among each group of churches, to pledge support for their missionary, and to send him out to reach those lost peoples.

One student at the school who was not pastoring a church received the missionary call to the Waudzungwa tribe from the

Udzungwa Mountains located in the south central region of Tanzania. Our pastors had caught the vision of reaching all the tribes of Tanzania with the saving Gospel message of Jesus Christ. There was a holy excitement in our midst and everyone was praising God for a renewed fervor for reaching the lost. In addition to the Waudzungwa, the other unreached tribes targeted were the Wazaramo, a Muslim tribe on the coast, and a largely unreached section of Wamaasai.

By the next term, one group had raised funding from among their group of local churches and an agreement was made to send out a missionary. He worked for one year in the region and many lives were changed by the Gospel.

The Holy Spirit had firmly planted in Terry's heart to further investigate unreached tribes in Tanzania. There was a new stirring of the Holy Spirit—a destiny moment for Terry. In the 1980's, during a season of fasting, Terry had received this scripture from the Holy Spirit: *For the vision is yet for an appointed time, but at the end it shall speak, and not lie: though it tarry, wait for it; because it will surely come, it will not tarry.* (Hab. 2:3 KJV) When he received that verse, he was a young man in his thirties, in the early years of preparation as a faculty member at Liberty University. Twenty years later, using the Bible knowledge he had gained from sitting under the teachings of anointed speakers from all over the world such as: Rev. John R. Rice, Rev. Jerry Falwell, Dr. Francis Schaeffer, Dr. Harold Wilmington, Dr. Ed Dobson, and many others, God was about to launch him into the ministry opportunity of a lifetime.

Using insights gained during his first safari into the bush to locate the Barbaiq and Hadzabe, Terry was spiritually charged for the second missionary journey to the Yaeda Valley. By faith he went believing God for another miraculous encounter with the Barbaiq—the only tribe feared by the Maasai.

The second journey in Terry's own words: *It is Friday and I have returned from my missions trip into the bush. The whole trip was a miraculous blessing from start to finish, thanks to the extensive prayer support from all of you. Certainly I want to let you know that I am safe and well, but that does not even begin to touch the miraculous outcomes of this trip to the Hadzabe and Barbaiq. Thank you so much for your prayers. We will begin to report all about the many wonderful things the Lord did during this trip in more detail in a newsletter that we will begin working on today. However I must tell you about one of the truly amazing events of the trip.*

Perhaps you will recall that in a previous newsletter I told you about how, on a trip into the bush in February, we gave a lift to a Barbaiq man who was walking alone out in the middle of nowhere. In talking with him, it turned out that he was the nephew of a Barbaiq man that Pastor Nanyaro knew from 25 years ago. We learned the name of the village where this man was living and the general area where it was located. So on this recent trip we headed out asking God for divine guidance and to connect us with key people who could help reach the Barbaiq people. After driving several hours out from Manyara, we stopped to ask a man alongside the road if he ever heard of this village. It just so happened that he had married a woman from this village and knew its location. After some discussion he agreed to guide us through the bush to the village. It also just happened that the very place one would turn off the road to go to this village was only about 50 yards from where we just happened to stop to seek directions! So off we headed for several more hours over mountains and through rivers (getting stuck only once for just a little while—thank God for Land Rovers with diff-lock) and we arrived at the village which was spread out over a large area. Again, we passed a Barbaiq man walking. We stopped the car and asked him if he knew Gilexa. "Yes, he is my father, and I am on my way to his house!" We gladly gave him a ride and arrived at the house of Gilexa Gasenovu. It turns out that in the intervening twenty-five years, Gilexa had risen to become the richest and most influential leader of the Barbaiq. He had eight wives, living on eight different bomas, hundreds of cattle, and had served as the chief elder of the Barbaiq for many years. Certainly the Lord had led us to the right man, but this was a pagan man, and now the Lord needed to touch his heart.

Having learned the importance of relationships and mutual understanding from dealing with the Maasai over the years, we took the time to talk with Gilexa over a period of several days. I asked Gilexa if he believed in God. "Of course, a person only has to look around to see that there must be a God," he answered. He told us the name for God in Barbaiq is "Ased." I told Gilexa that all over the world, people know that Ased created the world and all that is in it. In fact, Ased wanted people to know all about himself so he spoke to men and had them write down his story in the Book of the Words of Ased. I told him that as we talked we would explain things that Ased had written in His Book. Gilexa thought this was a good idea. When asked if the Barbaiq have holy men, or priests, or witch doctors, he said they have one such person who is the spiritual chief called the Gutamin (not a name, but an office, a high priest of sorts). We talked about how people have nature to do wrong/bad things and Gilexa understood this. In Swahili the word we use to describe such things is dhambi (i.e., sin). Gilexa understood that dhambi separates man from the favor of Ased. I asked Gilexa if the Barbaiq have ways to restore favor with Ased for dhambi, and he explained two ways depending upon whether the dhambi involves a family member or some other kind of dhambi. In both cases, forgiveness for dhambi involves the sacrifice of a sheep, and usually a "lamb!" In one case, the blood of the lamb is placed on the tip of a spear and the person seeking forgiveness licks the blood of the lamb. In other words, it is through the blood of a sacrificial lamb that the Barbaiq seek forgiveness from Ased. I asked Gilexa why they used a lamb, since cattle were the most important thing in their culture. He said he didn't know; it had always been this way. I asked Gilexa if making these sacrifices changed people so that they would not commit dhambi. He said no.

Then I explained to him that Ased, in His book, from the very beginning required the shedding of blood of a lamb for the forgiveness of dhambi. The Word of Ased explained that although sacrifices covered the dhambi, and made man aware of his nature to commit dhambi, that man would continue to commit dhambi because his heart was not changed. However Ased had a solution to the problem of dhambi—all explained in the Book of the Words of Ased. Ased sent his Son to earth to pay the penalty for the dhambi of all men. His Son's name was Yesu (Swahili Jesus). In fact, in the Book of the Words of Ased, Yesu is called the Lamb of Ased. Yesu, the Lamb of Ased, gave his own life, shedding his blood as a sacrifice to pay the penalty for the dhambi of all *people. But Ased did not allow Yesu to remain dead. He brought Yesu back to life, showing all people that He was indeed Ased and that Yesu had power over death and dhambi. Then Ased took Yesu to heaven and made Yesu the Gutamin over all peoples for all time. Ased, in the Book of his Word, explained that from then on, man would no longer sacrifice a lamb for the forgiveness of dhambi. Instead, because Yesu, the Lamb of Ased, had shed his blood, men could receive forgiveness for dhambi and receive the gift of eternal life in heaven with Yesu by simply believing that Yesu had given his life to pay the penalty for their dhambi and that Ased had raised him back to life. If one believed this in their heart and simply told this to Yesu and asked him to forgive his sins, Yesu would not only forgive him, but the Spirit of Ased would come and live in his heart, changing his heart and giving him victory over dhambi. By simply believing in what Yesu had done, one could not only receive forgiveness for his dhambi but could receive a changed heart that would enable him to live a life of victory over dhambi and thereby receive the love and peace and joy that all men seek through the power of the Spirit of Ased who would come and live in his heart.*

Gilexa said that he knew in his heart that these words were true and that Ased had sent us and that he received these words from Ased. When I asked him if he would like to pray and tell this to Ased and to ask Yesu to forgive his sins, he said of course—a man would be foolish not to receive the Word of Ased. Then he raised his hands toward heaven and prayed and said he believed in what Yesu had done, and he asked Yesu to forgive his sins and to come and live in his heart. Hallelujah! He said that for his whole life he had done many things, stealing cattle, fighting the Maasai, drinking Pombo (beer), but from this day on, he only wanted to tell his people about Yesu. Then he said, "You must come and teach us about the Words of Ased." We, of course, said that we would. Then we told him about our school where we study the Words of Ased and we asked him if he could find some Barbaiq men to come and study with us, then we would return with them to teach the Words of Ased. He said that he would find these men.

We agreed to return to the village in August (after the Bible school terms in Moshi and Manyara). We explained briefly how he should pray daily to Ased in the name of Yesu for his family, his home, his cows, his friends, etc. This truly was a divine appointment which I know God will use to reach the Barbaiq. We can't thank you enough for your prayers. Please continue to pray for Gilexa and that God will provide students from the Barbaiq and the Hadzabe. The trip was so miraculous from beginning to end that we know the Lord was responding to your prayers. There is so much more we would like to tell you, such as the equally divine connection with the Hadzabe. But we must close for now.... Thank you, thank you, thank you, for your prayers. There is rejoicing in heaven today! Gilexa Gasenovu, chief elder of the Barbaiq, husband of eight wives, former warrior and cattle thief, is truly a son of Ased!

The ministry to the Barbaiq was the most challenging we had ever undertaken. But because we had learned much from our strengths and failures when reaching out to the Maasai, we were able to proceed with more wisdom. The Maasai culture had presented many problems for ministry. Taking the Gospel message was just the first part of the Great Commission. Jesus also commanded us to teach them to obey the things He taught. To the Maasai people, polygamy is the norm. That alone presented all kinds of problems. Specifically in 1Timothy 3, polygamy would seem to preclude a man with multiple wives from being a pastor, elder, or deacon. Yet Jesus clearly taught against divorce! Should a man with more than one wife be permitted to attend Bible school? What about the wife of such a man, could she be qualified to serve as a deacon, pastor or elder or to attend Bible school?

How to handle these situations were thoughts that frequented missionary moments around a cup of *chai*. The first missionaries had drawn a hard line on the issues early in their teachings and for a while we didn't address the issue. But once we were involved with the Barbaiq, it became *our issue*. We needed to hear from God about it and draw godly conclusions. The Bible states in 1 Tim 5:8, *if anyone does not provide for his relatives, and especially for his immediate family, he has denied the faith and is worse than an unbeliever.* (NIV) The King James Version calls that one an infidel—hard words, but a worthy saying. A wife put out would take her children and all of them would be like Hagar in the desert—totally destitute with dire consequences until God showed up. It was now time for us to be His rescuers for those about to be in need of rescue. In the New Testament Jesus never said anything about polygamy, but He said a lot about faithfulness in marriage. And He sure spoke against divorce! These were tough issues, and something had to be done to protect innocent lives from destruction. Anytime a person is born again and becomes a child of God, he or she enters into that relationship with cultural baggage from the past. Sometimes it takes generations to work through all the baggage in order to bring culture into a closer alignment with the Word of God.

During this time we received a wonderful letter from a former missionary to South America. In her letter Dr. Lila Robinson encouraged us to not teach the Barbaiq to put their wives out. That choice could only lead to one of two consequences: starvation or prostitution for survival. By the time we received the letter, praise God, we had, by the Spirit, come to the same conclusion. It was a great confirmation! We had indeed heard from God. Our decision was to encourage them to not take any more wives, but to continue in their responsibility of providing for the ones they already had along with their children. According to Paul's words to Timothy, it was the only truly Christian thing to do.

Elders were the traditional way of guidance in the villages. Anything that smacked of defaming them or causing them shame by stripping them of their traditional role would destroy the potential of the work in progress and any future prospect of reaching out to the people. In civil village matters, it was status quo. As far as church leadership, we needed to look to the second generation for trained leadership. But anyone and everyone should be allowed to study God's Word. Jesus made new creations, never second class citizens.

Spiritually it was the most oppressive season of our lives. The enemy's attacks upon us personally were numerous and varied. It was a wearing down tactic of the devil to rob our peace and joy. During this time we experienced an inside robbery from trusted people aimed at stealing the satellite phone given to us by our friends, Ralph and Jo Anne Feith. That phone was critical for Terry to remain in communication with me from the bush in case of vehicular failure or any other crisis situations. Mission Aviation Fellowship could then have been alerted for an emergency evacuation. Later the phone was miraculously recovered. An Asian (person from India) friend of Brian's called him when an accomplice of the thief tried to sell the satellite phone to him. The shopkeeper merely confiscated it. Things work differently and more simply in third world countries.

My personal challenges involved the 12 long hours alone at home between sunset and sunrise when Terry was in the bush. Those lonely nights were the nights when it seemed the darkness got darker. Sometimes when Brian was also out of town doing ministry, Janine would come over and we would spend the nights together. Under the safety of the mosquito net, we would pray and then laugh together watching a *Hogan's Heroes* video on a laptop until slumber would come. She was like a *Ruth* to me! Those were the fun, secure nights. But most nights, not only did the electricity go out, neither guard would appear, and every other unimaginable weird thing would happen—like a water pipe bursting or our guard dogs getting suddenly sick and the vet could not be contacted until morning. Usually it was a combination of several of those. It was bad! No it was worse than bad; it was diabolical!

After a bit of panic on my part, I would eventually—sometimes hours later—calm down. Once again I would realize my circumstance was no surprise to God. And no matter what the enemy had planned for me, God would take care of me— whether here or in heaven. Especially on those nights—I proclaimed my trust in the God of the Bible who said—*And they overcame him (the devil) by the blood of the Lamb and by the word of their testimony, and they did not love their lives to the death.* (Revelation 12:11) Then surrendering afresh, I would just say something like, "Jesus, please surround the compound and my bed with Your holy angels and cover me with Your blood." Then I opened my Bible, read it until peace came, placed it open on my chest, and sleep all night. That gesture was merely a demonstration in the natural of my belief in the power of God's living Word in my life. 1 John 4:18 says *but perfect love casts out fear, because fear involves torment.* My learning to love and trust God completely, no matter what, was the only thing that could bring His peace into my world and end the tormenting fear of the unknown.

Standing on the truth of God's Word was my defense in the war for my mind. If I didn't guard my spiritual heart, the enemy would attempt to take a foothold there. When Terry was away on his monthly trips into the bush, the Barbaiq and Hadzabe territorial spirits would attack me viciously. It was an unseen war—a battle for the souls of men, and the demons were determined not to relinquish their influence in the lives of those people.

As Terry's monthly ministry trips continued the presentation of Jesus as the sacrificial Lamb of God so touched the hearts of the Barbaiq elders that they readily responded when they heard the Gospel. This was necessary, because the elder men controlled everything in the village. With the Maasai it has been difficult to reach the elder men, but among the Barbaiq, God had touched the elder men first. In our past failures with Maasai church plants, the Maasai women readily embraced the Gospel, but for the Maasai men, it became a women's movement. The men wouldn't get involved—even beating the women for attending service. A hard lessoned learned—the cultural significance of reaching the village elders first. Any other method would end in disaster.

Because Barbaiq culture centered on livestock, especially cattle, Nanyaro's veterinary skills and Terry's microbiology background were the perfect combination to diagnose and treat their sick cattle. Again it turned out that most of their sick cattle had a tick borne disease called *babesiosis* which Terry diagnosed by using his microscope. The cattle clinic drew a crowd. After about half a day of ministering to their sick livestock, the men were willing to sit and listen to the missions team talk about their reason for being there—to tell them about Jesus.

Until that day, the fledgling church among the Barbaiq had only one member, Gilexa Gasenovu, the first convert, who was around 80 years old. It was critical for the continuation of what God had begun in the Yaeda Valley to find younger Barbaiq men to train to be Gospel warriors. The salvation of the Barbaiq tribe depended upon it!

These people had never heard about Jesus. When Nanyaro began explaining to two men that we came to talk about Jesus, one man pointed to Terry and asked, " *Is he Jesus?*" Another said he heard of religion, but who was this Jesus? With the help of Gilexa and the cattle clinic, finally a few men were willing to come to Bush Bible Camp under the tree and talk about Ased (God). Next to the tent and the campfire was a shade tree where classes were held. Over the course of four days again they presented Jesus as the Sacrificial Lamb of God who came to take away the sins of the world. Four hungry men remained the entire week; others came and went during the teaching. One day Jesus was introduced as the Lamb of Ased (God). The second day focused on repentance. The third day Terry explained what it meant to be "born again." Finally, on the fourth and last day, the class learned about the Holy Spirit, His indwelling presence, and empowerment for believers. Since people were coming and going all the time, much reviewing was necessary each day. At the end of the day the teachers and class would kneel under the tree and pray together. By the end of the week, seven men had repented, confessed their belief in Jesus, prayed to receive Him as their Savior, and received the filling of the Holy Spirit! Among those saved was another very old and influential elder, and the administrative officer of the village of Endanyawish, a government official who stopped by to check out the *Wazungu* and ended up staying and receiving Christ.

As a result of the four-day Bush Bible Camp, the new church grew to eight men including Gilexa. This work was unique in that it began entirely with the salvation of the Barbaiq eldership—necessary in the male dominated society. Surely this was a God-ordained work! The last act of the school was to pray for the anointing of the Holy Spirit on them, and commission them to go tell!

During another visit to Endanyawish, Terry and Nanyaro realized a big problem had ensued among the young men. In Terry's own words: *We realized that the young men (between the ages of 13-25) were not coming to our meetings and were not receiving Christ. When they did stop by our meetings under the baobob tree, they didn't stay very long. During our last visit, however, several young men came and stayed the entire day hearing teaching from the Bible on repentance. At the end of a day, we always give an opportunity for those present to respond to the Word. When these young men were given an opportunity to pray to receive Christ as their Savior, they began to talk among themselves. Thinking that perhaps they didn't understand, we went back over the Gospel message and gave them another chance to respond. Once again, no response! This was very unusual. Although we didn't understand their lack of response, we closed in prayer for the day.*

Since it was rapidly becoming dark, we built a fire and prepared some food and tea. While we were eating, one of the young men returned and said that he wanted to explain their behavior. He said that they understood that they needed Jesus, but they also understood that they needed to quit sinning! Since none of them had killed their elephant yet, and since killing elephants is illegal and therefore a sin, they would have to wait until after they killed their elephant to receive Christ. Further discussion that evening and the next day revealed that in fact every Barbaiq "boy" must kill an elephant with a spear in order to become a "man." Until they become a man, they are not allowed to even talk to a girl, let alone speak to her father about marriage. So these men are planning an elephant hunt after the rains. It was encouraging that the older men recognized this was a problem and began to discuss possible solutions. They were beginning to take ownership in their church.

The Lord and His Gospel Warriors had won a great battle among the men in the Yaeda Valley, the Valley of the Barbaiq!

Another sort of battle raged for the Barbaiq, Christianity had become a men's club—no women allowed! Gilexa and the others weren't even telling their wives about Jesus. It was at this time that Terry announced to them, "I won't help you build a church until you tell the women!" Finally one of the men, Daktari, who had come to the Bible school under the tree shared the Gospel with his wife. Daktari was a radically changed man! He insisted that the three of them—Terry, Nanyaro, and Daktari take the two hour walk into the bush to share the Gospel with his mother. Daktari understood; his eyes were opened. He even tried coming to *civilization*—the LMCC campus—but he was so uncomfortable in the strange surroundings and fearful for the welfare of his cows he left. But this he knew—he needed to share the Good News with all his people bound in Barbaiq the religious tradition of worshipping the ancestral spirits.

Tribal peoples live in fear of offending the ancestral spirits. The witch doctor uses these fears to manipulate the people. After the salvation of the some of the first Barbaiq women, the witch doctor visited them. He put such fear in them that they recanted of their new found faith in the Living God. Then out of their intense fear, they gave the witch doctor a goat, which he sacrificed to appease their ancestral spirits.

Despite the aggressive actions of the witch doctor, Terry continued to move forward and scheduled a baptism. *You are of God ... and have overcome them, because He who is in you is greater than he who is in the world.* (1 John 4:4 NKJV)

To celebrate this glorious occasion we invited our special friends, Gregg and Robin Dokka, from Clearwater, Florida to come and minister with us. Dr. Gregg, our anointed chiropractor, had done much to keep our necks and backs moving and our joints free from pain. He had definitely been one of God's instruments for our longevity on the field. Robin, his wife, is a tremendous prayer warrior who had interceded for us for years. We wanted them to witness the miraculous things that God was doing in our midst.

While the men were on safari to Yaeda Valley for a three-day off road ministry camping trip, Robin and I were to do the second women's conference with the ladies from the Manyara region. All of us were greatly anticipating the things the Lord had in store for us.

Robin and I were excited to be sleeping at the Lake Manyara Bible School in the new guest quarters. After arriving at the school, we immediately went inside to make up our bunks, arrange our mosquito netting, and prepare our lessons. The compound was awfully quiet for a conference day. That seemed very strange, for the ladies usually arrived early and began to joyfully sing and pray with great zeal. I couldn't understand where everyone was! Later, as I descended the steps from the guest room to check things out, I noticed Mama Veronica sitting at a desk in the grassy area between the dormitory and classroom buildings. She was collecting names and handling money. Now even more puzzled, I looked inside the classroom building. Inside I saw very few women. The last conference had almost six hundred in attendance—even the prostitutes came. In the past I had some concerns about some financial issues, but this time there was no mistake. Something was not right, and I wanted to know what was going on. Clearly, Mama Veronica was charging entrance fees for the conference.

I couldn't believe it! No one would have the money to come. Poverty, as always, was rampant in the region, but this year it was worse. The rains were insufficient; with severe drought, the harvest was minimal. On top of that rats had invaded the countryside, eating everything in sight not destroyed by the sun. The rat infestation had taken an enormous toll on the economy. They even broke into the storage room of Lake Manyara Christian College and ravaged all the plastic plates and cups and even the plastic Thermos tops. With the rats came another episode of bubonic plaque infecting the neighboring community of Karatu. Fortunately, that all preceded our visit.

So as Terry talked with Pastor Nanyaro about the conference, he mentioned that I had sent two hundred dollars for Veronica, his wife, to use as "she thought best." All this was while they talked about the conference. For Terry it was totally implied— this was to be used exclusively for the conference needs—food, plates, firewood, sanitary products, etc. Having done a conference there before he assumed Nanyaro knew the drill. As usual we intended to feed everyone a healthy lunch. In addition this year we even needed to purchase new plates—no thanks to the rats!

Translation from one language to another can be very challenging to relationships. When the men were talking about the poverty and the conference, naturally Terry assumed that Brother Nanyaro would understand the money had been sent for the conference. When I confronted her about charging the impoverished women, immediately she was on her cell phone telling her husband, Nanyaro, to get over here—*sasa hivi*—

right now! Pastor Nanyaro and I had a lengthy, painful discussion. Let's just say Mama Nanyaro was the best dressed woman at the conference!

The situation grieved me deeply! God had something profoundly anointed awaiting the women of Manyara, and none of them were even here to receive it. At times like that I seemed to forget that the situation was no surprise to God; He was still on the throne! At that moment I had a choice to make. Either I could allow my anger and disappointment from one misunderstanding rob the anointing and all Jesus wanted to do, or I could forgive and move on—right then that very moment! I made the decision the cross demands and moved forward. I called Terry and somehow we got another two hundred dollars and the conference went on. It was a tough lesson for all of us.

Finally, when the announcement was made that the conference was free, the building began to fill. We concentrated our teachings on women's issues and marriage and family. Robin, the mother of three, was delegated to teach on disciplining the children in the home. She had begun her teaching by telling the women the biblical importance of disciplining their little ones. As she spoke, the Holy Spirit quickened me to warn Robin to be specific in describing exactly what she meant by discipline. This she did well, for at testimony time a woman shared, *"Thank you for teaching me how to discipline my children. Now I won't bite them anymore!"*

The conference continued, but things between Veronica and me were never the same. True repentance never came. It was the "I am sorry I was caught" rather than a changed heart attitude. Women's conferences were amazing educational tools not only for the Tanzanians, but also for this mzungu. During each woman's meeting God had something in store for me. No matter what I was teaching, I was the one learning the most!

From my experience, greed manifesting itself in money matters or theft destroys more missionary and national relationships than anything else. From that moment on, every cent designated was more carefully scrutinized. Even before that day we had required documentation for all purchases. Money received was signed for; receipts were required. Clarity and accountability bring peace, promoting integrity and trust. And accountability thwarts the enemy's attempts to bring division.

I was so grateful Robin was there to pray for me and with me through this difficult experience. Letting go was not easy. Although I had made the right choice to move forward, my anger kept trying to resurface. It was a battle of the will. *"Be angry, and do not sin": do not let the sun go down on your wrath, nor give place to the devil.* (Eph. 4:26-27 NKJV)

After saying farewell to the Dokkas we returned to Moshi.

Haunted by the Hadzabe

Living alongside the Barbaiq in the isolated area southeast of the Serengeti near Lake Eyasi, are the pygmy-sized Hadzabe (hawd-zaw'-bay). The two tribes coexist peacefully because the kali (fierce) Barbaiq are herdsmen and the Hadzabe are hunters and gatherers.

These primitive hunters and gatherers continue to live in their ancient ways and speak a click language similar to the Bushmen of the Kalahari. The Hadzabe are omnivores with a diet including wild fruits, nuts, berries, roots and various game meats. Each member of society is responsible for specific food types; the men are the hunters and their women the gatherers. During the day Hadzabe women gather available varieties of vegetation. Cautiously they limit the quantity of roots removed—to not endanger the life of the plant. Specific roots and barks are valuable herbal medicines—each disease-specific.

On the other hand Hadzabe men basically hunt anything that moves, from very small hares to huge giraffe and elephant. Their handmade weapons are bows with four differently designed arrows, each one animal-specific. To three of the arrows poison is carefully applied; sources vary—one variety is from snakes and the other two varieties come from poisonous plant extracts. Following the arrow's lethal injection, the men track the animal until it dies. Immediately after finding the carcass, a runner is sent off to gather the women. Together again they butcher the meat, and carry it back to their family *kiota* (Swahili for nest).

These nomads do not keep any livestock, plant crops, or build homes except for large hay mounds used during daylight hours to provide relief from the intensity of the equatorial sun. At night they sleep under the protection of trees in a human-size nest made of grass. A misguided cultural belief is that if their children sleep in a building under a roof, they will die. A typical sleeping group consists of a one man and a woman with children and maybe some older parents. Beside the common Tanzanian problems of malaria, worms, and other parasites, the Hadzabe people are plagued by diseases of the chest such as bronchitis and pneumonia due to their constant exposure to the elements. As Terry traveled into the bush to visit the Hadzabe, he would always take along life saving supplies of antibiotics to distribute.

The Hadzabe are a spiritual people who worship a god named Hyine (hi-een'-ay) and the spirits of their ancestors. Monthly, during the darkness of the new moon, they gather to worship the pagan gods. On this diabolical day they offer a child sacrifice to receive direction from the gods for the hunt. Pastor Lazaro once commented about this horrible practice, *"The child is not stolen. Willingly the parent gives the child considering it an honor to have his child chosen."* Ignorance of God's Word perpetuates the darkness of their society.

Ironically, their spiritual understanding includes a spirit known as the devil—they just need to be taught the evil of his ways. Previous evangelistic attempts among the people centered on church buildings in the small towns surrounding the land of the Hadzabe. Western religious culture didn't facilitate their nomadic way of life. Attempting to be sensitive to the Hadzabe culture, we began to pray to ask God to give us a few Hadzabe to train and work with at the Bible school. God gave us the plan to train up those Hadzabe men and place them out in the bush where the people were rather than in towns.

We needed anointed Hadzabe men willing to embrace their nomadic lifestyle. The tribe was spread out, didn't live in houses, and spoke the most difficult language. We believed the Holy Spirit gave us a plan to train five Hadzabe pastors for a circuit walking bush ministry. As God provided the funds, we would establish a central mission station where the pastor could live with his wife and children. From that strategically located mission station, the pastor would go out by foot making a weekly or biweekly circuit ministering to and teaching the Hadzabe in his area. One such station that was sponsored by Faith Chapel, Syracuse, New York became the base of operations for Pastor Issak.

Thus the victory we all celebrated in 2005 when the first Hadzabe arrived at Bible school. Issak came dressed in the traditional clothing, a garment draped over the shoulders and tied at the waist, flip flops, and his weapons in hand. Issak embraced the call of God in an incredible way. He received Jesus as Lord while we were studying the Pauline Epistles. Sensing from the Holy Spirit that He was about to do something wonderful, I took an extended period of time to explain God's plan for the redemption for mankind from Philippians, chapter 2. Issak had a real *aha* experience as he came to realize this Jesus left the glories of heaven, became a man, and suffered, just like him and for him. This Savior also walked dusty roads ankle deep in dirt mixed with dung and debris. Like Issak, Jesus was alone and rejected, hot, thirsty, hungry. With his spiritual understanding opened Issak, brave Hadzabe hunter, literally jumped out of his seat and ran forward and to kneel down to receive Jesus as his Savior! He came before the invitation was even given. I stood in absolute awe of God's grace and mercy for what He was doing to bring these people out of ancestral worship and related diabolical deeds. Later, while I was praying for the sick, Pastor Nanyaro called the other two Hadzabe men forward to ask if they were ready. Both said a resounding YES! But as they began to pray, Melchizedeki was unable to speak. He tried but nothing would come out. Something was wrong. After a quick prayer seeking guidance from the Holy Spirit, I noticed that he was wearing a strange necklace with many weird religious symbols on it. Mentioning the discovery to Pastor Nanyaro, he immediately took action and requested that Melchizedeki remove it. After removing the religious relics, the young man's mouth was opened and boldly he accepted Jesus as Savior. Three more Hadzabe now had their names written in the *Lamb's Book of Life!*

Melchizedeki become an outstanding student, being the only one to get a perfect score on one of Terry's quizzes. The second week of school, Manassas came. He testified that last year an evangelist came and he had repented from drunkenness and fighting. He was now committed to take the Gospel to his people.

Trying to establish a firm foundation, the five Hadzabe students were kept for an additional week of discipleship following the July 2005 term of the Bible school. They were taught from our extensive yet condensed Swahili discipleship course designed for nurturing new believers. The week culminated with a march to the river for a glorious water baptism for the three Hadzabe most recently saved. All five now had been born again, baptized, and were ready to begin to minister among their people—we thought. We divided all of the Hadzabe land into six regions. Our five students were ready to be placed in four of those six regions to begin taking the Gospel to their own people.

Any safari—even by 4X4—to the bush can be dangerous as there are no real roads and the dirt tracks are really more like bad footpaths. Quickly trouble can arise! Such was the situation when Terry and Nanyaro were delivering the Hadzabe students in their designated areas of ministry. The first thing that happened was that the starter on the truck stopped working. Not a big problem as long as there were men to push-start it or a hill to coast down.

In order to shorten the trip and cut off about 50 miles and a couple of hours, they made a decision to cut across the grassland instead of following the dirt track. The grass had been grazed back to about an inch by the wildebeests and gazelles; it appeared they could see all the way across to the mountains about ten miles away. At first it seemed really great sport driving along through the herds of wildebeest. Then the grass started getting higher–little by little. Also, the soil began getting softer. Terry shifted into diff-lock and kept going. Before long the grass was up to the hood of the Land Rover Discovery, and the earth continued getting softer and softer. Terry increased speed to prevent the truck from getting bogged down in the muck soil. Suddenly the grass was up to the roof and visibility was absolutely zero! The cool short cut across the valley jogging with the wildebeest had suddenly become a white knuckle prayer time!

As they were plowing blindly through the grass, the dangerous conditions increased as the soil steadily kept getting softer and softer. With the starter also nonfunctioning, excitedly Nanyaro cautioned Terry, *"Whatever you do, don't let the car stall!"* Attempting to push the car in the soft boggy soil would be impossible. The terrified passengers began to cry out to the Lord in Swahili, *"Please Lord, keep us from getting stuck! Please Lord, don't let the car stall! Please Lord don't let us hit an elephant!"* The only sound heard was the grass smacking against the car and the people inside praying.

After what seemed an eternity, they finally broke out of the grass onto the other side. As the soil began getting firmer, they shouted in unison, *"Asante Yesu!"*—"Thank you, Jesus!"

Later with the last student dropped at his home on the other side of the grassland, they continued up the valley until they came to a dry riverbed. As they started across, the car bogged down into the sand. The more Terry tried to accelerate the Discovery, the more the tires continued to dig into the sand— the hole got deeper and deeper. Again Pastor Nanyaro reminded Terry, *"Don't let it stall!"* With the car running, the men disembarked. Quickly they began digging out from around the wheels and replacing stones for sand under the wheels to build a stone track. After almost an hour of road building on the dry river bed, they were able to push the vehicle onto the stones and drive it out of the river. Fortunately they had enough petrol!

After returning to Bible school the next term, Manassa became very ill. He was sick with fever and needed immediate treatment; we sent him to the clinic. Our obvious conclusion was a bad case of malaria, but we just wanted to be sure before we began treating him. However, his fever was a result of two STDs. He had syphilis and gonorrhea. His infidelity had several disastrous life altering consequences. The disease had passed to his pregnant wife, who gave birth to a child blinded by the gonorrhea infection. Certainly a tragic sin, but was it beyond God's grace if he repented? No! Spiritually was he exhibiting character traits mature enough for the task ahead? No! Every single day in East Africa, sexual sin destroys lives. We grieved deeply for Manassa and his family—especially the blind baby boy whom he named Brian after our son. Surely if he had heard the Good News and met Jesus as a young child, his tragic life could have been different!

Another sad disappointment was Melchizedeki, who had agreed to the evangelistic plan, but later preferred the easy life around Yaedachini (more like a primitive Wild West town) and refused to get "bush dirty." When the Hadzabe came to school, they were freezing in the higher elevation so we bought shoes and warm clothes for them. Melchizedeki decided to remain in the city with his new shoes and clothes. He didn't want to be dirty anymore. In such poverty that we Westerners could never fathom, it does not take much for the enemy of our souls to deter a man from God's purpose.

In scripture, of course, we find that Hadzabe's noble name, Melchizedek, associated with the Prince of Salem, who brought out bread and wine for Abraham as he offered tithes to

237

Melchizedek, meaning my King is Righteousness. His falling short only reminded us all the more of the need for sharing the Gospel of Grace with those who need to know the Prince of Peace.

Issak remained faithful for the longest period—about eighteen months. His ministry was powerful. One day Issak and Nanyaro ministered to a woman living in a nearby *kiota,* who had been blind since she was a little girl. As they prayed for her, she was miraculously healed. Instantly she received Jesus as her Savior! Her testimony led many to Christ. People were leaving the traditional religious church and coming over to fellowship at the mission station where the power of the Holy Spirit was meeting with them.

One day a local religious leader went to meet with her. Immediately after the evangelist of that church shared a cup of tea with her she fell over dead. Poison kills more than animals in bush culture. About this same time famine hit the land so severely that all the animals left. With no resources for food, Issak took a job with a safari company as a hunting guide. Could it be he was also intimidated by the death of the woman? Fear can paralyze even the strongest of saints. Over the next two years he would periodically call and say he would be returning to school after the next hunt. Then there would be one more hunt. Finally when he was completely ready to return, he had taken a second wife and Pastor Nanyaro refused to admit him. If the devil couldn't destroy them one way, it was another.

A Shocking Banana

Morning in Tanzania was an amazingly beautiful time. Multicolored birds nestled in the hedges sang peacefully as the rising sun warmed their bodies. Yellow sunrays reflected from the glistening glacier surrounding the volcanic cone on the top of Mount Kilimanjaro. Our compound was surrounded by a bougainvillea thorn hedge decorated by vibrant purple, magenta, and salmon-colored paper thin flowers. This was the view from the sunroom, our favorite devotional place. Suddenly overtaking the peacefulness would be the loud, deep honking of the Hadadah ibis as they passed over our compound each morning. Then peace would come again.

The nights were often noisy and full of disturbances, whether it was thieves on the road or the nearby female guard dog in heat—dogs barked and barked and barked throughout the night until the local roosters took over sometime after three AM. After the continual racket from the night before, peace in the morning was a soothing necessity. And, indeed, this fateful day the morning was peaceful for the moment.

The two Maasai warriors dressed in their full red battle regalia had finished their sunset to sunup shift of approximately twelve hours. The warriors had been hired to protect us and all our stuff from thieves. They proceeded in their normal exit routine. First they would lock up our two German shepherd guard dogs. Esther and Timothy were penned behind the workers' quarters under the shade of red banana trees purchased from an old Chagga *bibi* (grandmother). Each day for a week she walked down the steep mountain slopes of

Kilimanjaro to our compound on thickly callused bare feet. Skillfully she balanced a banana tree on her head each day. We paid her a dollar a tree; she was blessed and so were we! Terry loved those big thick red bananas and the dogs loved the coolness of the banana leaves. There they gladly rested after an exhausting evening of tearing from one side of the yard to another barking and barking. Midnight madness for them was the excitement of chasing and catching wild screeching hedge hogs. The guards were usually sound asleep somewhere, occasionally even in a tree, and never heard the dogs. Eventually I would wake up Terry. Flashlight in hand he would unlock all the many doors and security grillwork to exit the house and rescue the hedgehog. The prickly varmint would then be placed in a bucket and gently thrown over the fence with the hope that it had learned its lesson—no frolicking in this yard!

Another frequent nighttime disturbance was the neighborhood guard's whistles, which woke up everyone. Whistles of fellow guards immediately got our Maasai guards' rapt attention! A blasting whistle meant a thief had been spotted. Instantly, all the guards began sounding their whistles to alert the other nearby guards. This also scared off the thieves, who understood everyone was now awake in the neighborhood!

With the dogs asleep, the guardsmen would lock up their bows and arrows, hang up their whistles, fill a bucket of water to bathe, and, finally refreshed, would turn the compound gate key over to Robert, the day guard and gardener. Robert arrived as they exited. Guards were a necessary part of the economy.

Often the system reminded me of the old Mafia insurance schemes we saw in films.

Until the year 2009 when firearms found their way to Moshi, we were still secure in this primitive spot in the universe because the word was out we had the locally dreaded Maasai guards. The Maasai are noted warriors, even able to kill a lion with the swift swing of their hardwood knotted club. The clubs were tucked under their belts which were also helpful in keeping their plaid red robes together. A Maasai warrior on duty demanded instant respect among thieves. These guys were trained killers. That fact alone was a form of protection. Having a club, a spear, and a bow with arrows made them a formidable defense. In addition, Terry would occasionally hold archery practice with them in the yard where the hedge was thin. This exercise was specifically designed to give the entire neighborhood a view of our skillful guards and their *mzungu* boss. The warriors loved challenging the *mzungu* to target practice. Yohanna, our first Maasai guard who is now a pastor with a flourishing bush church, had arrows specially made for us by a local bushman tribe. Yohanna's family used these same arrows for protection from the local marauding elephants determined to destroy his family's *boma*. But our guards' weapons were now in lockup waiting for darkness to return again.

We loved that one hour of solitude and peace with God. The sunroom was located just off the kitchen. Most mornings were begun there meditating on the Word and discussing the day's agenda. Terry always needs at least two cups of coffee to get his body into motion; while on the opposite end of the spectrum, I bounce out of bed ready for action. After Terry made his coffee, he settled into his chair in an attempt to wake up. He was reading as I exited the kitchen. He was getting himself prepared mentally and spiritually for a day in town. A day in Tanzania usually required a big infusion of God's strength and courage!

The day before I had begun to experience some rumbling intestinal symptoms, so that morning I had taken a tablet to relieve symptoms of amoeba or giardia. As missionaries, we had little control over foodstuffs prepared outside of our own home. Intestinal issues plagued us after we drank tea made from water not boiled at least fifteen or twenty minutes or ate anything that was not cleansed properly. At home, all our fruits and vegetables were soaked in a water and *Jik* solution for twenty minutes. Then to remove the bleach flavor, the items were rinsed with sterile water. Locals did not follow this procedure as their normal intestinal flora could seemingly handle anything but the ever present parasitic worms.

Time is something westerners allow to rule their lives, but most village people live for the moment. Wristwatches were luxury accessories more than a time piece for village folk. So anytime we were in a village or at a pastor's house where the food or water were not sufficiently boiled or cleansed, we were sick—and that was often. But that was only one way it challenged us. Amoeba could also attack us just because we breathed at the wrong moment. Amoebic cysts were in the air. Maasai cows grazed everywhere on Moshi's dirt roads. Under the powerful equatorial sun, cow manure quickly dried and became part of the particles in the air. Whenever a car would speed by, billows of dust would envelop us as we walked along the roadways. We would then breathe it into our lungs or it would come in our windows and rest upon our tabletops, pillow cases, and everything else. Each day more dust could collect upon our tabletops than we would see in one year at home. Hidden within the dust was an invisible pollutant with a very painful physical result. Keeping the house and floors dust free was a full-time job. That is certainly one of the main reasons missionaries hire house workers to help prevent reoccurring illnesses. Those unpaved roads constantly presented a problem. Our son, Brian, was the one who coined the phrase, "The roads are like dry river beds." We all bounced up and down, gully after gully, necks jerking backward and forward in a whiplash-type action again and again, rocking and rolling, swaying back and forth all at the same time. A local joke, not too funny actually, went something like this: "How can you tell if it's a giraffe or a rabbit on the road? If you can see the ears, it's a giraffe." So true! During and after the rainy season people would be stuck clogging along with shoes caked in mud inches thick. Four wheel drive vehicles were a necessity. Then as soon as the rains were done and the sun came out, the dust returned in no time at all. But those four to five days of dust-free, muck-free roads were heavenly.

For my stomach pains I tried a different medicine that I had never taken. The reaction was potentially lethal. Immediately, I began to feel woozy and actually began to walk like a drunken sailor as I entered the sunroom. I started laughing in a silly manner. I said to Terry. "Something is wrong, but I didn't have a stroke." He yelled to me, "You better sit down before you fall down." Even as he finished the last phrase he instinctively knew something was dreadfully wrong and sprung to his feet and caught me mid-air as I began to fall onto the bright orange ceramic tile floor. He scooped me under my arms just in time as my legs gave out. By the time he got me in bed, I could no longer walk. Speedily, steadily I was losing muscle control from my feet upwards. As I lay in the bed, he frantically began looking for Benadryl tablets. Finding one he gave it to me immediately. Moments later I told him it was getting more and more difficult to breathe. Frantically he searched the cupboard for another and somehow God gave me the strength to tell him where we had one more left in the travel bag from our last safari to the bush. By the time he gave me the second one my lips could no longer form around the cup. I could hardly swallow the water. It was dribbling down over my face and chin, soaking the pillow case. Then I told him to call Brian. I knew he would pray in faith, and what I needed then was prayer. It was a miracle his cell phone was on as he was at his church office for morning prayers. His custom during this hour was to turn it off. He sped toward our home in record time, stopping momentarily to check and see if anyone was staffing the local clinic and to alert them that he and Terry would be bringing me over as I was experiencing a reaction to meds. In the meantime, I asked Terry to call my dear friend Anne Street, a nurse. She arrived quickly and listened to my heart and took my pulse. She began to intercede for me and cried out to the Lord on my behalf. Later she told me that when she arrived she didn't know if I could make it as my body was shutting down so dramatically fast. As soon as Brian arrived they carried me to his Nissan Patrol. Terry held my arms and Brian gathered my legs and together they put me into the vehicle. I could hear

Brian praying powerfully and rebuking the spirit of death, for surely I was dying inch by inch as my body shut down—feet, legs, chest, lungs, and lips—but my mind was sharp and clear. Our workers were panicked as they looked upon the scene.

The reaction at the clinic was much the same. The receptionist immediately began to cry. Later she told Janine that she was shocked to see Mama Weaver, who was always so full of energy and joy, lifeless. Getting herself under control, the nurse helped place me on a gurney and I was ushered into the treatment room by the head nurse. Immediately Dr. MaCupa began questioning me. "Mama Weaver, do you know who you are? Do you know who I am? Do you know where you are?" All of these questions I was able to answer correctly, but it was difficult to speak. My voice was very soft, almost inaudible. I could tell the muscles controlling my breathing were about to shut completely down. I almost had no energy left to speak. I lay helpless, but totally peaceful. There was absolutely no fear! I knew my life was in the balance between earth and eternity, but I knew the One who had control of that fragile balance. It was the Lord God Almighty! Only He would and could determine the outcome of this battle of life or death. Jesus, our Healer, had preserved my life. Many circumstances were in place for my survival: my loving husband, Terry, was at home rather than in the bush; our beloved son, Brian, had forgotten to turn his cell phone off; my dear friend Anne came immediately and began to intercede; the medical clinic was only two compounds away and was open and had exactly what I needed to stop the reaction. Now that alone is a miracle in a third world country! Most importantly I live because Jesus lives. He is the Living God, the Giver of life now and forevermore. Again He showed Himself to be the faithful God. For many years we had this verse on a note stuck to our mirror, *For the eyes of the LORD run to and fro throughout the whole earth, to show Himself strong on behalf of those whose heart is loyal to Him.* (2 Chron. 16:9 NKJV) Indeed He was strong for me that day.

But I will sing of your strength, in the morning I will sing of your love; for you are my fortress, my refuge in times of trouble. (Psalm 59:16 NIV)

As I was writing this portion of our life in Tanzania, I was sitting in an allergist's office waiting for the results of my allergy tests. Funny thing—it was discovered I am severely allergic to bananas—our African mainstay. Trip to the bush—take the bananas. Dessert—bananas, snack—bananas, when in doubt, eat a banana. We ate a lot of bananas every day. They were a perfectly safe fruit totally enveloped in a protective covering. A sure thing not to make you sick! Hmmm… perhaps it was a combo of the drug and the morning banana that almost did me in! But God!

Home Again: More Culture Shock

The Word of God declares *whereas you do not know what will happen tomorrow. For what is your life? It is even a vapor that appears for a little time and then vanishes away.* (James 4:14 NKJV) One day we were missionaries and the next day we knew our time in Tanzania had to be over! Done! Such a sudden ending of what had been for over a decade a valiant attempt in Jesus' mighty name to withstand the forces of evil and accomplish for God what could only have been possible with Him at the helm. Did the devil win when allergies diminished my capacity to exist in East Africa, or was it just God's way of saying enough?

In all honesty, I believe the latter could be the case. The pressures of the warfare the last couple of years were enormous. We had invaded the enemy's territory, and we paid a huge price. Certainly it was nothing in comparison to what it cost the Savior, but we had become weary warriors.

In the beginning years of our ministry, we were going where many of the territorial strongholds had been demolished by the prayers of missionaries who had gone before us. Although there remained battles to engage with victories to be won, the final years were just different. Terry was compelled by the Spirit to enter the Yaeda Valley, the homeland of the Hadzabe and Barbaiq. It was a God-given assignment, but the devil wasn't about to just move over and make room for the Gospel. For generations the people groups there had been bound; the devil was not about to give up, just unchain them, and invite the Gospel into that dark, dark place. The Valley of the Barbaiq and Hadzabe was virgin territory—a completely different situation. Our prayer warriors and we were the pioneering forces pushing back the forces of hell. Powerful, wicked spirits inhabited the land. What could be more wicked than a controlling territorial demon demanding child sacrifice? At the new moon, deceived hungry hunters/gatherers offered their own flesh and blood to appease the gods for hunting direction. Those dominant controlling demons fought back in ways we had never experienced. Unseen forces worked overtime to amass stress upon stress. We were exhausted spiritually under the pressure.

Oswald Chambers reminds us that *"the process of being made broken bread and poured out wine means that you have to be the nourishment of other souls until they learn to feed on God. They must drain you to the dregs…. Before other souls learn to draw on the life of the Lord Jesus directly, they have to draw on it through you; you have to be literally 'sucked' until they learn to take their nourishment from God. We owe it to God to be the best for His lambs and His sheep as well as for Himself."* (February 9. *My Utmost for His Highest*) We were absolutely spent—sucked dry. Chambers' wise words remind me that it's okay; that's how it works. Now was the time to release the LMCC disciples, as years before we had released the KCC disciples to find their nourishment directly from the Spirit of God.

I had actually begun praying for my life—acknowledging to God I just couldn't live like that anymore. Daily on my knees, previous to the allergy attack, I had been asking—no, begging—God for deliverance from the magnitude of the oppression. How it came was a shock, but the answer was clear. It was time to go home. This chapter in our lives was complete.

God had already set in motion the continuation of His work. *"Not by might nor by power, but by My Spirit,"* says the Lord of Hosts. (Zech. 4:6 NKJV) A school for training leaders from the region was in place. Because of the sacrifices of many and the manpower of two upstate New York churches, Faith Chapel, Syracuse, and Full Gospel Community Church, Warsaw, Lake Manyara Christian College had been built. God had brought us a righteous man, Danieli. He was a redeemed Barbaiq man from another area who heard the Macedonian call to move into the region. The Barbaiq built him a home, but his wife refused to move because of the lack of water. In Africa, water seems always to be a problem—too much or too little, usually too little. We offered to purchase a donkey cart and barrels for Daniel to get water once a week from a source half a day's travel away. He decided against this solution.

In 2008, a year after we left Moshi for America, Terry together with a team from ZAO Water, in association with Morningstar Ministries, returned to the valley of the Barbaiq to drill a well for the region. The drilling process was exhausting, challenged at every point. Even the temporary living conditions were almost unbearable for many.

Water is necessary to keep the drill moving. As the drill bit penetrated the rock and dirt, the water would bring the debris to the surface and remove it in the form of slurry. When the water the drill team had trucked in ran out, Pastor Danieli and Terry first drove thirty minutes to the elephants' watering hole and emptied it by using buckets. With that depleted, next they travelled two hours each way to the dry riverbed and dug down about four feet by hand to get enough water to continue. They filled the 55 gallon drums one cup at a time.

Because of the distance off road, the team had elected to purchase plastic casing rather than extremely heavy steel. After days of challenged but successful drilling, the plastic casing smashed at the final moments at the depth of the well when going through the final strata of rock. There was no way to retrieve it.

A brutal climax; all involved were devastated. With Barbaiq culture centered on cattle; the vision for watering holes and cattle tick dip situated by the church were put on hold. It seemed the *perfect* plan to draw cattlemen to the water then teach them about the Living Water. Lastly, without water Danieli has chosen not to move to the deserted place. But he remains committed to taking the Gospel to the valley. Periodically, he travels two days coming and going from his home by bicycle to minister to the church. He graduated from Lake Manyara Christian College in November 2010. May God grant him the grace to finish the race in the strength of the Holy Spirit.

Pastor Nanyaro continues to disciple the Christian men and women in the Lake Manyara region. Pastors Lazaro and Eli Kiriama continue to serve the Lord at Kilimanjaro Christian College and also as part of the national leadership of PEFA. Our Maasai *sons,* Longida and Yohanna, continue to pastor in separate isolated bush regions among their own people. They are in the process of planting more churches in other villages among the Maasai. Hundreds have graduated from the two Bible schools and hundreds more will continue to come, be trained using our materials, and then be sent out. Recently we learned former students from the Evangelistic Assemblies of God in Tanzania have shared our KCC course-books with others. Hearing the call of the Great Commission, they have gone out and planted a Bible school in a Muslim region along the coast of Tanzania. My prayers for multiplication of fruit continue to bring a harvest. God had raised up national missionaries to carry on the Great Commission in our stead.

In December 2009 we moved to Virginia Beach to be nearby our children and grandchildren. Brian had become a pastor at New Life Providence Church and Janine was a student at Regent. We became local grandparents and helped as needed while Janine finished her education. Our son, Eric, his wife, Liz and our granddaughter, Olivia Grace were only three hours away in Charlottesville, Virginia. Our life was full and wonderful.

There were days when I longed for the beauty of Tanzania—its people, the powerful ministry, the magnificence of Mount Kilimanjaro in the distance. Writing this manuscript helped to bring God's peace and rest to my soul as layer after layer of repressed memories and pain were uncovered and healed as necessary repentance was offered and God's forgiving grace cleansed my soul. God's mercy gave me a new level of freedom. Our lives had changed only by location, not vision. From 2007 to today we continue in service to the Living God— writing, teaching, or preaching. When He opens a door, we walk through it. Some doors can be closed for a season and then when least expected can begin to open again.

Recently God has begun to stir our hearts with renewed missionary fervor. It began late in the fall in 2011when God spoke to my spirit and said, "I am about to *expand your horizons.* Recently I heard *"Get your house in order I am about to move you."* Brian and Janine are also on the move again and will be heading to Germany with their two children, Abigail Marianne and Nathaniel Joshua.

We are not yet sure what fully lies ahead as we surrender afresh to the Spirit's call. But of this we are certain—having our destiny attached to the King of kings is a very safe place to be. In my heart I would love to occasionally return to Tanzania to interact with the men and women we had previously trained. Maybe even another Bible School for Women for those who were just children or young mothers before. The same God who healed my back can deal with my allergies; there is a new level of faith arising in me. And, of course, Terry's heart's desire would be to see the Barbaiq well flowing with God's life giving water—the kind that nourishes one's body, soul, and spirit. Terry is excited about the possibility of teaching in Germany, the land of his ancestors if the Lord chooses to open a door there. Hmm, and Tanzania is only one jet ride away from Germany. Could there be a sequel to *Jambo, Kilimanjaro!* or perhaps *Guten Morgen, Germany*?

For in Him we live and move and have our being.

(Acts17:28 NIV)

Epilogue

Living in the past with regrets or even longing to return to places that were once fruitful can be unproductive both mentally and spiritually. Learning to live in the *now* is exciting. Our Lord's mercies are new every morning. Keeping our ears attentive to the cry of His heart opens the way for new adventures in Him. New seasons of life can produce abundant fruitfulness through us if we are only willing to be open to the *new thing* that God wants to do in us and with us in spite of our age! Amazing things can happen when we heed God's voice to, "Go!" Timothy, Abraham, Deborah, and Moses are examples of biblical leaders of every age seasoned with God's salt and purged in the fire of life who said, "Yes."

Yes is the operative word that the Lord is waiting to hear from us regardless of our age or the talents we think we have or don't have. God wants us to be willing to be open to receive whatever the Holy Spirit is saying and doing right now.

Recently, while teaching on Lot's wife, I was reminded how paralyzing it can be to incessantly be looking backward. Instead of being continually out there sprinkling salt in our culture, we can become stagnant, even useless, if we don't stay open to the Holy Spirit's cry to arise. Lethargy is the plague of humanity without God—not those with God!

It's time to take back what the enemy has stolen and arrest his advancement wherever we are—our family, our neighborhood, and our country. It's not about location; it's about passion for the souls of humankind. That which is a priority to our Father must be important to us. It's time to reenter the fight for God's kingdom here and abroad. We need to get His strategy and engage the battle.

Daily we are to be taking up the cross and moving forward toward that goal. Truly God is calling His people out of complacency to open themselves to more of Him and less of us. We are to be moving from glory to glory as our lives become more and more surrendered to God's purpose for us in Christ Jesus. The same Spirit that raised Christ from the dead lives in us; get connected—and get going! Now is the time. Just say yes!

Even when I am old and gray, do not forsake me, O God,

till I declare Your power to the next generation,

Your might to all who are to come. (Psalm 71:18 NIV)

Let's pray, *"Lord have your way and may my life ever be a YES before you. Amen."*

Glossary

Asante—thank you

Asante sana—thank you very much

Boma— an enclosure or compound

Bwana— title for males: mister, sir, or Lord in reference to God

Chai—tea

Choo—a Tanzanian toilet (*vyoo* plural)

Duka— a shop of any kind

Elim—Elim Fellowship in Lima, New York

Ghali sana—very expensive

Hatari—danger

Hamna shida—no problem

Iraqw—the tribe in the Manyara/ Karatu region

Jambo!— Hello!

Jik—a bleach product

Kanga—a vibrantly decorated square cloth used for many things: a head covering; a shawl; a skirt; or a carrier for baby or produce.

Kali—fierce or sharp

Kairos—opportunity

Karanga—peanut

Kiota—nest

Maasai boma—a compound of one or more huts for one family or an extended family enclosed by stacked thorn bushes for protection from predators.

Matatu—overcrowded mini bus usually driven recklessly

Musth—a period of increased hormones in bull elephant resulting in aggressive behavior

Mzungu—white person or person of European descent

PEFA—Pentecostal Evangelistic Fellowship of Africa

Punda milia—zebra literally meaning striped donkey

Shida—problem

Vigelele—a loud noise made by saying *la* rapidly

Vyoo—plural of choo

Wameru—the Meru people group living in Mount Meru region

Warusha—the Maasai people group living in Arusha area

Wazungu—plural of mzungu; more than one white person or person of European descent

Made in the USA
Charleston, SC
28 April 2012